NUREG–1150
Vol. 3

Severe Accident Risks: An Assessment for Five U.S. Nuclear Power Plants

Appendices D and E

Final Report

Manuscript Completed: January 1991
Date Published: January 1991

Division of Systems Research
Office of Nuclear Regulatory Research
U.S. Nuclear Regulatory Commission
Washington, DC 20555

ABSTRACT

This report summarizes an assessment of the risks from severe accidents in five commercial nuclear power plants in the United States. These risks are measured in a number of ways, including: the estimated frequencies of core damage accidents from internally initiated accidents and externally initiated accidents for two of the plants; the performance of containment structures under severe accident loadings; the potential magnitude of radionuclide releases and offsite consequences of such accidents; and the overall risk (the product of accident frequencies and consequences). Supporting this summary report are a large number of reports written under contract to NRC that provide the detailed discussion of the methods used and results obtained in these risk studies.

This report was first published in February 1987 as a draft for public comment. Extensive peer review and public comment were received. As a result, both the underlying technical analyses and the report itself were substantially changed. A second version of the report was published in June 1989 as a draft for peer review. Two peer reviews of the second version were performed. One was sponsored by NRC; its results are published as the NRC report NUREG-1420. A second was sponsored by the American Nuclear Society (ANS); its report has also been completed and is available from the ANS. The comments by both groups were generally positive and recommended that a final version of the report be published as soon as practical and without performing any major reanalysis. With this direction, the NRC proceeded to generate this final version of the report.

Volume 3 of this report contains two appendices. Appendix D summarizes comments received, and staff responses, on the first (February 1987) draft of NUREG-1150. Appendix E provides a similar summary of comments and responses, but for the second (June 1989) version of the report.

CONTENTS

TABLES

APPENDIX D

RESPONSES TO COMMENTS ON FIRST DRAFT OF NUREG–1150

CONTENTS

D.1 Introduction*

The previous draft of NUREG–1150, "Reactor Risk Reference Document," was issued as a draft report for public comment in February 1987. At that time, a notice was published in the *Federal Register* announcing the availability of the report and requesting comment (Ref. D.1). Distribution was made to approximately 850 people or organizations in the United States and abroad.

To assist readers of the document, a 2-day seminar was held in April 1987 on the methods used in the risk analyses of draft NUREG–1150. A notice of this seminar was sent to all persons receiving the draft report and published in the *Federal Register* (Ref. D.2). The seminar took place in Rockville, Maryland, and was attended by 173 people from various organizations, including Federal agencies, State agencies, utilities, architect/engineering firms, and consulting firms.

In response to the request for comments, the NRC staff received 55 letters from 45 authors totaling approximately 800 pages. The authors of these letters and their affiliations are listed in Table D.1. All letters received are available for inspection in the NRC Public Document Room.

In addition to these reviews and comments, draft NUREG–1150 was reviewed by three formal peer review committees. Two of these reviews were initiated by the NRC; the third review was initiated by the American Nuclear Society. Also, as part of the normal review process within the NRC, the staff discussed the methods and results of draft NUREG–1150 with the Advisory Committee on Reactor Safeguards on several occasions (Ref. D.3).

1. Review by Kouts Committee

One of the major advances of the risk analyses discussed in draft NUREG–1150 was the performance of quantitative uncertainty analyses. The specific approach used to perform these uncertainty analyses was reviewed by a panel of five experts, chaired by Dr. Herbert Kouts of Brookhaven National Laboratory. The members of this committee are listed in Table D.2. The committee performed its review from April to October of 1987. Its findings were published as Reference D.4 in December 1987.

2. Review by Kastenberg Committee

The NRC invited Professor William Kastenberg, University of California at Los Angeles, to form and chair a committee to peer review the entire breadth of risk analyses, as documented in draft NUREG–1150 and supporting contractor reports. Lawrence Livermore National Laboratory was funded by NRC to provide technical and administrative support. The members of the committee, listed in Table D.3, were selected by Professor Kastenberg. The committee performed its review from June 1987 to March 1988, with its findings published as Reference D.5 in May 1988.

3. Review by American Nuclear Society

The American Nuclear Society (ANS) chartered a special committee chaired by Dr. Leo LeSage of Argonne National Laboratory to study and critique draft NUREG–1150. The members of this committee are listed in Table D.4. The committee started its work in the fall of 1987 and published its findings as Reference D.6 in April 1988.

4. Overview of Comments and Responses

It is the nature of reviews of documents such as draft NUREG–1150 that extensive comments are received and that most of the comments are critical. Before discussing the principal (negative) comments, it is worth describing the principal positive comments that were expressed in letters and committee reports:

• It is believed that the NUREG–1150 study is the first comprehensive treatment of both modeling and data uncertainty in risk. In prior PRAs, the accounting of uncertainty has been limited to data uncertainties.

---

*This appendix was published in the second draft of NUREG–1150, reflecting comments on the first draft report (1987). It has not been modified for this (final) version of NUREG–1150 except for updating the reference list.

Table D.1 Authors of public comment letters.

Abe, K.	Japan Atomic Energy Research Institute, Japan
Artigas, R.	General Electric, San Jose, CA
Booker, J. E.	Gulf States Utilities Company, St. Francisville, LA
Boyer, V. S.	Philadelphia Electric Company, Philadelphia, PA
Brons, J. C.	New York Power Authority, White Plains, NY
Butterfield, L. D.	Commonwealth Edison, Chicago, IL
Caisley, J.	Organisation for Economic Co-operative Development/Nuclear Energy Agency (OECD/NEA), Paris, France
Campbell, R. M.	Massachusetts Voice of Energy, Boston, MA
Chubb, Walston	Murrysville, PA
Cogne, F.	Institut de Protection et de Surete Nucleaire, Commissariat a l'Energie Atomique, France
Colvin, J. F.	Nuclear Management and Resources Council, Washington, DC
Cullingford, M.	International Atomic Energy Agency, Vienna, Austria
Edwards, D. W.	Yankee Atomic Electric Company, Framingham, MA
Gardner, R.	Stone & Webster Engineering Corporation, Boston, MA
Gridley, R. L.	Tennessee Valley Authority, Chattanooga, TN
Hayns, M. R.	United Kingdom Atomic Energy Authority, Culcheth, United Kingdom
Hiatt, S. L.	Ohio Citizens for Responsible Energy, Inc., Mentor, OH
Hintz, D. C.	Wisconsin Public Service Corporation, Green Bay, WI
Hobbins, R. R.	Idaho Falls, ID
Hockenbury, R. W.	Rensselaer Polytechnic Institute, Troy, NY
Hoegberg, L., et al.	Swedish Nuclear Power Inspectorate, Sweden
Janecek, R. F.	BWR Owners' Group, Chicago, IL
Khobare, S. K.	Bhabha Atomic Research Centre, Bombay, India
Kingsley, O. D., Jr.	System Energy Resources, Inc., Jackson, MS
Kowalski, S. J.	Philadelphia Electric Company, Philadelphia, PA
Kranzdorf, R.	San Luis Obispo, CA
Langley, J. R.	Mark III Containment Hydrogen Control Owners' Group, St. Francisville, LA
Lash, T. R.	Illinois Department of Nuclear Safety, Springfield, IL
Levenson, Milton	Bechtel Western Power Corporation, San Francisco, CA
Lewis, M. I.	Philadelphia, PA
Liu, K. C.	Atomic Energy Council, Taipei, Taiwan
McNeill, C. A., Jr.	Public Service Electric and Gas Company, Hancocks Bridge, NJ
Myers, R.	Clean Air Council, Philadelphia, PA
Newton, R. A.	Westinghouse Owners' Group, Pittsburgh, PA
Reiman, L.	Finnish Centre for Radiation and Nuclear Safety, Finland
Sholly, S. & Harding, J.	San Jose, CA
Soda, K.	Japan Atomic Energy Research Institute, Japan
Spangenberg, F. A., III	Illinois Power Company, Clinton, IL
Speelman, J. E.	Netherlands Energy Research Foundation, Netherlands
Stewart, W. L.	Virginia Electric and Power Company, Richmond, VA
Taylor, J.	Electric Power Research Institute, Palo Alto, CA
Tucker, H. B.	Duke Power Corporation, Charlotte, NC
Vaughan, J.	Department of Energy, Washington, DC
Warman, E. A.	Stone & Webster Engineering Corporation, Boston, MA
Zaffiro, C.	Energia Nucleare e delle Energie Alternative, Rome, Italy

Table D.2 Members of Kouts Committee.

Herbert Kouts, Chairman	Brookhaven National Laboratory
Allen Cornell	Stanford University
Reginald Farmer	Consultant, United Kingdom
Steven Hanauer	Consultant, Technical Analysis, Inc.
Norman Rasmussen	Massachusetts Institute of Technology

Table D.3 Members of Kastenberg Committee.

William Kastenberg, Chairman	University of California, Los Angeles
George Apostolakis	University of California, Los Angeles
John Bickel	Northeast Utilities
Roger Blond	Science Applications International, Inc.
Simon Board	Central Electricity Generating Board, United Kingdom
Michael Epstein	Fauske and Associates, Inc.
Peter Hoffman	National Nuclear Research Center, Federal Republic of Germany
Frank King	Ontario Hydro Company, Canada
Simon Ostrach	Case Western University
John Reed	Jack R. Benjamin and Associates, Inc.
Robert Ritzman	Electric Power Research Institute
John Stetkar	Pickard, Lowe and Garrick, Inc.
Theofanis Theofanous	University of California, Santa Barbara
Raymond Viskanta	Purdue University

Table D.4 Members of ANS Special Committee on Reactor Risk Reference Document.

Leo LeSage, Chairman	Argonne National Laboratory
Edward Warman, Vice Chairman	Stone and Webster Engineering Corporation
Richard Anoba	Carolina Power and Light Company
Ronald Bayer	Virginia Power Company
R. Allan Brown	Ontario Hydro, Canada
James Carter III	International Technology Corporation
J. Peter Hosemann	Paul Sherrer Institute, Switzerland
W. Reed Johnson	University of Virginia
Walter Lowenstein	Electric Power Research Institute
Nicholas Tsoulfanidis	University of Missouri
Willem Vinck	Consultant, Belgium

- The methods developed during the study are desirable because uncertainty can be quantified, the contribution of various sources of uncertainty can be determined, the net impact of hypothetical design changes can be assessed, and important technical issues can be identified.

- It is believed that the basic methods used to generate the risk distributions are sound.

- It is believed that important advances made in severe accident analysis since the last major risk study, the Reactor Safety Study (Ref. D.7) done in 1975, are reflected.

- The detailed models of events and phenomena that load a containment and the response of the containment structure using event trees place added emphasis on the importance of the containment function. This seems desirable.

- It is believed that a reasonable approach was used to represent the capacity of a containment with technical issues about the failure pressure, failure location, and failure size and including interdependencies among the various phenomena.

- Engineering judgment was used when data were unavailable. Gaps in the understanding of severe accident phenomena were represented with technical issues and used as a means of investigating various hypotheses of severe accidents. This is believed to be acceptable and may be the only way to advance a risk assessment.

- Past risk assessments were reviewed to identify previously uncovered subtle interactions among components with formal investigations thereafter. This is a desirable practice because it takes advantage of previous work.

Most of the critical comments on draft NUREG-1150 were on four broad subjects. Some of them were attributable to technical deficiencies in the risk analyses while others were related to inadequate documentation. The four major areas of concern pertained to: (1) methods that were considered to be inadequate for obtaining and using expert judgments; (2) information that was considered to be outdated; (3) calculations that were considered to be inscrutable; and (4) results that were considered to be improperly presented or displayed. These areas are discussed in Sections D.3.2, D.3.3, D.4.1, and D.4.3 below.

It should be noted that some comments addressed potential new and long-term research programs, especially in the area of severe accident phenomenology. Such comments are not discussed here.

In the following sections, the comments received on draft NUREG-1150 have been grouped into seven major topics: (1) objectives and scope; (2) overall methods; (3) tracing and documenting calculations; (4) accident frequency analysis; (5) containment loads and structural response; (6) source terms and consequences; and (7) regulatory uses of NUREG-1150. With the large number of comments received in each of these areas, it was not possible to list and respond to individual comments. As such, individual comments on similar subjects have been paraphrased and responses then made to these paraphrased comments.

D.2 Objectives and Scope

D.2.1 Objectives

Comment: Clear objectives should be established and explained for NUREG-1150, and the report should be focused on those objectives.

Response:

The objectives of NUREG-1150 have been reviewed and clarified in response to comments on the draft report. These objectives are outlined in Chapter 1 of this report; they are:

- To provide a current assessment of the severe accident risks of five nuclear power plants of different design, which:

  - Provides a snapshot of risks reflecting plant design and operational characteristics, related failure data, and severe accident phenomenological information available as of March 1988;

  - Updates the estimates of NRC's 1975 risk assessment, the Reactor Safety Study;

  - Includes quantitative estimates of risk uncertainty in response to a principal criticism of the Reactor Safety Study; and

- Identifies plant-specific risk vulnerabilities for the five studied plants, supporting the development of the NRC's individual plant examination (IPE) process;

• To summarize the perspectives gained in performing these risk analyses, with respect to:

- Issues significant to severe accident frequencies, containment performance, and risks;

- Risk significant uncertainties that may merit further research;

- Comparisons with NRC's safety goals; and

- The potential benefits of a severe accident management program in reducing accident frequencies; and

• To provide a set of PRA models and results that can support the ongoing prioritization of potential safety issues and related research.

Comment: The manner in which the results of NUREG-1150 are to be used in the regulatory process should be discussed.

Response:

Since the publication of draft NUREG-1150, the NRC staff has developed an integration plan for regulatory closure of severe accident issues (Ref. D.8). In this plan, the role of NUREG-1150 is described as one of the principal supporting resource documents to this regulatory closure process. Further discussion of the uses of NUREG-1150 is provided in Chapter 13 of NUREG-1150.

D.2.2 Scope

Comment: The scope of NUREG-1150 is narrowly defined, making the risk study incomplete. Many types of accident initiators are unaccounted for, including earthquakes, floods, and other external events; reactor coolant pump seal failure; steam generator tube ruptures; and instrument air losses. Other phases of plant operation need to be considered in addition to normal full-power operation, including power ascension and descension; shutdown; and operation with Mark I containment buildings de-inerted. Accidents in spent fuel pools should be taken into account.

Response:

The scope of the current version of NUREG-1150 has been expanded to reflect comments made on the draft report. An improved reactor coolant pump seal LOCA model has been developed, and steam generator tube ruptures have been explicitly considered. As in the draft report, the effect of failures in supporting systems (ac and dc power, instrument air, auxiliary cooling water systems) has been included in the system fault trees. In addition, external events have been included in the analyses for two of the plants (Surry and Peach Bottom) to determine the core damage frequency and containment performance associated with a range of external initiators. The NRC staff intends to evaluate the significance of external events at the remaining plants in a later study, currently scheduled for completion in FY 1990. With these changes, the staff believes that NUREG-1150 presents an adequate representation of the risk associated with the five plants analyzed, subject to the constraints established by the state of the art of probabilistic risk analysis.

To confirm that the scope is appropriate, the NRC is initiating a separate study of the risk associated with low power and shutdown conditions for two of the plants studied in NUREG-1150. The results are expected to be available in FY 1990. The risk associated with spent fuel pool accidents is being assessed separately in studies responding to NRC's Generic Issue 82, "Beyond Design Bases Accidents in Spent Fuel Pools." When completed, these will be examined to determine if further efforts are advisable.

Because of the small fraction of time that the BWR Mark I containment is de-inerted during startup and the approach to shutdown conditions, compared to the length of the operating cycle, and the small frequency of accidents occurring in these times, the NRC does not intend to further study the risk implications associated with de-inerting.

Comment: NUREG–1150 should take credit for accident management strategies to reduce the likelihood of a core damage accident or to mitigate its consequences.

Response:

Both the draft and present versions of NUREG–1150 explicitly consider the effects of plant operational procedures to provide water and cooling to a reactor core to prevent its damage. Procedures for performing such actions are obtained from the specific plant under study. These are reviewed to assess the probabilities of successful use in associated accident scenarios. These probabilities are then incorporated into the accident frequency analyses for that plant.

The present version of NUREG–1150 also incorporates the effects of plant operational procedures on mitigating the consequences of core damage accidents. Procedures in place at the individual plants were used to assess the probability of successful operator action.

Comment: Accident sequences with frequencies below 1E–7 per year have not been considered. Events at 1E–8 or 1E–9 per year might be significant, either individually under particular conditions or cumulatively when many such sequences are excluded.

Response:

Given a set of initiating events, event tree/fault tree analysis like that performed for NUREG–1150 permits the examination of logical accident sequences. The trees were quantified by calculating each branch to its end; when a branch frequency fell below a cutoff frequency, it, and hence the accident sequences it represents, were excluded from the analysis. The cutoff frequency used in the present version of NUREG–1150 is 1E–8 per year for internally initiated events, which is sufficiently low to retain more than 95 percent of the accident sequences contributing to the core damage frequency. However, in several instances accident sequences with a frequency below these levels were explicitly included to ensure adequate representation of a wide spectrum of accidents.

D.3 Overall Methods

D.3.1 Uncertainty Analysis

Comment: The treatment of uncertainty is questionable and inherently biased. The large uncertainty bands and high risk estimates may result from the methods used; uncertainty in variables may have been combined without compensating to prevent many variables from realizing worst case values. Other methods exist for quantifying uncertainty, such as the Optimistic/Central/Pessimistic (OCP) method and sensitivity studies.

Response:

The Latin hypercube sampling (LHS) method used in NUREG–1150 is a form of Monte Carlo sampling, an algorithm for sampling from individual parameter distributions and, based on the risk model, combining these individual distributions into a single distribution. More generally, such sampling is known as mathematical experimentation and is used in other disciplines (Ref. D.9). This mathematical experimentation is used to propagate uncertainty through large mathematical functions that preclude propagating uncertainty analytically. The validity of the results is dependent upon the validity of the assumptions made about the distributions of the variables. The displays of risk may give the impression that the risk estimates are rigorous classical statistics but they must be taken in context, realizing the strengths and the weaknesses of the methods used to compute the estimates and the underlying data base.

LHS was favored over the OCP approach on the basis of theoretical grounds and the potential of each method. Probabilistic techniques constitute a theoretically sound and standard technique for combining uncertainties; the LHS framework contains a basis for implementing such a technique. In contrast, the OCP framework requires that a series of pessimistic or optimistic assumptions be combined without quantifying the likelihood that the combination of assumptions could arise.

The LHS algorithm for generating Monte Carlo samples is one that has undergone extensive review in the open literature and is used both in the United States and abroad. The estimators of LHS are unbiased when the variables are uncorrelated. Bias may occur when the variables are correlated, but this is a characteristic of Monte Carlo sampling in general and not a characteristic of LHS.

Some specific aspects of the use of LHS in draft NUREG-1150 had the potential to introduce bias. In the draft report, the uncertainty in individual parameters was represented in a discrete manner. Because such use may cause bias, the discrete parameters were replaced with continuous parameters for the present version of NUREG-1150. Because the methods used to obtain expert judgments and to formulate distributions based on the judgments can introduce bias, formal methods designed to minimize bias were used in the present risk analyses. This is discussed in greater detail in Section D.3.2.

As noted in the Introduction, the treatment of uncertainty in draft NUREG-1150 was reviewed by a peer committee; their findings are published as Reference D.4, and all their major comments have been incorporated in the present analyses.

Comment: The conclusion that the uncertainties have increased over a dozen years of research does not seem correct. NUREG-1150 does not portray the progress made in hardware modifications, operator experience, and research since the publication of the Reactor Safety Study (Ref. D.7) in 1975. Furthermore, the conclusions in draft NUREG-1150 are similar to those of the Reactor Safety Study, meaning that draft NUREG-1150 is inconsistent with almost every study published in the 1980's, all of which show a trend of lower estimates of risk. After a decade of severe accident research, it is unsettling to see risk results spread over several orders of magnitude.

Response:

It is clear that the technical information base on the frequencies and consequences of severe reactor accidents is substantially better now than in 1975 when the Reactor Safety Study (Ref. D.7) provided its analysis of risk and the uncertainty in risk.

In the Reactor Safety Study, the rigorous quantification of uncertainty was performed only for uncertainties in component failure rates. The overall uncertainties shown in consequences were developed by subjective judgments at a very coarse level. The peer review of the final version of the Reactor Safety Study, known as the "Lewis Report" (Ref. D.10), concluded that these uncertainty estimates were significantly underestimated.

The subjective uncertainty estimates developed and used in NUREG-1150 address uncertainties at a rigorous level and make extensive use of experimental and calculated results developed since 1975. Both the level and the basis improve the realism of the uncertainty analysis. These improvements are a direct result of an improved knowledge base (including the effects of phenomena not known in 1975) that permits a more accurate treatment and characterization of unknown parameters and modeling of physical processes. The large uncertainties simply reflect the state of knowledge in the severe accident area.

Comment: Uncertainty in offsite consequences was not factored into the risk estimates. This leads to misleading risk estimates.

Response:

With the exception of the variability of site meteorology, uncertainties in the consequence analysis have not been included in either the draft or present version of NUREG-1150 because of time constraints. The NRC staff recognizes that there are significant uncertainties in the consequence estimates due to uncertainties in modeling and in input data. Best estimate values of the model parameters for natural processes (plume behavior, deposition, etc.) have been used in Version 1.5 of the MACCS code

(Ref. D.11) for the current NUREG–1150 analysis. While the lack of accounting of consequence uncertainties can have an influence on overall risk results, it does not prevent the development of important perspectives on plant design and operation.

Some of the key parameters in the uncertainty of offsite consequence analyses relate to post-accident protective actions (e.g., emergency response and long-term countermeasures). That is, offsite consequences can be affected by the effectiveness of emergency response of the local population and by the radioactive contamination levels above which crops and land are removed (condemned) from public use. The sensitivity of consequences and risks to the protective actions is discussed in Volume 1 of NUREG–1150 and in References D.12 through D.16.

In addition to the risk studies of the five plants discussed in this report, the NRC staff is supporting the risk analysis of the LaSalle plant, a BWR–5, Mark II plant. It is planned that this risk analysis will include an analysis of the uncertainties in offsite consequences and the effect on risk estimates. This work is scheduled for completion in mid-FY 1990.

D.3.2 Expert Judgment

Comment: The protocol for obtaining expert judgment is not rigorous and yielded judgments with unsound bases. Technical subject areas should be kept separate, and experts should work within those areas (i.e., within their field of expertise). Panels should be composed of experts from all portions of the nuclear industry. The experts should be given a less restricted role in selecting and identifying uncertainty issues. Expert groups should interact to ensure that consistency is maintained throughout the analysis.

Response:

The protocol used to elicit and to aggregate expert judgment has been substantially improved for the present version of NUREG–1150 and is discussed in Section 7 of Appendix A. Standard and rigorous techniques were used; among the developers and the reviewers of the protocol were experts in diverse areas of uncertainty analysis and survey methods, including decision analysts, social psychologists, and statisticians from national laboratories, private companies, and universities. Seven groups of experts were established, each group working within a specific technical area. Each group included representatives from industry, academia, and the national laboratories.

For the current version of NUREG–1150, the experts were allowed to add issues to or delete issues from the list of issues presented to them. The context in which the issues entered the analyses was explained to the experts. The experts were encouraged to modify the statements of the issues to improve technical clarity and to define interdependencies among issues and between issues and other parameters in the analysis. The exchange of information between panels was effected primarily by the project analysis staff. The information exchanged concerned requirements for specific phenomenological information about an earlier phase of a postulated accident sequence that was needed to answer a question about a later phase of the accident.

Comment: Expert judgments are requested for inappropriate portions of the risk analyses. When adequate data exist to define uncertainty, expert judgment should not be used as a substitute. When little or no data exist, experts should not be asked to guess at distributions; instead, the particular uncertainty variable should not be included in the uncertainty analysis. No attempt should be made to quantify technical issues with expert judgments unless there is an adequate basis for that judgment.

Response:

For the present version of NUREG–1150, expert judgments were not used when available data were adequate to provide the required information. In some cases, such data became available during expert panel meetings, and issues were dropped from consideration by the panels.

While it is inappropriate to ask experts to simply guess at issue distributions, it is also inappropriate to exclude issues from consideration because of the scarcity of relevant data. Potentially important issues should be considered, even if the data are scarce and the basis for engineering judgment is very limited, because it is often the paucity of data that renders an issue an important contributor to uncertainty.

In technical areas where significant data existed, expert judgment still played an important role in ascertaining the relevance of the data to a particular application in the risk analysis. As an example, large uncertainties inherent in the models of containment performance precluded an accurate prediction of the location of failure under specific accident loadings. Various calculations of containment response were sometimes found to be conflicting, even when similar analytical methods were used. In 1987, at the Sandia National Laboratories, a scale model of a concrete containment was tested under conditions simulating a slow pressurization from steam and noncondensible gas generation from a severe accident (Ref. D.17). Organizations from the United States and abroad tried to predict the failure location and pressure. Only one of these predictions was close to the test results. For the purposes of NUREG-1150, the available data on both the experimental result and the reasons why calculated results differed were key to the assessment.

Comment: When distributions were assigned to variables, often high weights were assigned to the extremes of these distributions. This is unusual and should be justified. Integrated analyses based on models benchmarked against data would show that extremes could not be realized.

Response:

Documentation of the rationale for uncertainty distribution development, including the results of relevant code calculations and experimental results, was an important step in the elicitation process used in this report. This documentation is provided as Reference D.18. If high weights were assigned to the extremes of the distributions, then the associated documentation should provide the rationale. Discrete distributions were -replaced with continuous distributions to permit a better characterization of the uncertainties, particularly in the tails of the distributions.

D.3.3 Quality Assurance, Consistency, and State of the Art

Comment: A thorough review of the draft NUREG-1150 study is needed. The study does not appear to have been checked for inconsistent and meaningless results because some of the results are questionable or contradict results reported elsewhere in the same documents. The computer codes used in the risk analyses should be properly validated, documented, and peer reviewed, which also appears not to have been done.

Response:

The review of NUREG-1150 has been performed at two levels: an external level, including peer review and public comment on the draft report; and an internal review by the various organizations involved in the plant risk analyses. For the specific issues identified in this comment, internal review processes were used to ensure consistency and validity. This internal review had the following elements:

- **QA/QC Review of Principal Analysis Areas:** For each major area of analysis performed for the present version of NUREG-1150 (accident frequency, containment performance and source terms, offsite consequences), a QA team was established and the analyses were reviewed. This process for the accident frequency analysis is documented in References D.19 through D.23. Approximately 25 percent of the resources were spent on reviewing the work. The method was initially reviewed by a Senior Consultant Group, and then more detailed reviews were conducted by a Quality Control Team. These latter reviews occurred periodically over more than 2 years. In addition to the reviews that NRC and its contractors sponsored, the utilities involved have performed reviews and provided extensive comments that have been incorporated, as appropriate, into the analyses. This formal review process continued throughout the reanalysis effort. The modeling of core melting phenomena, source terms, and consequences as well as the risk analysis in the current version of NUREG-1150 were subject to a quality assurance review that is discussed in Appendix A to NUREG-1150.

- **Review of Computer Models:** A large number of computer codes were used in the performance of the risk studies described in this report. A number of them have been reviewed or benchmarked in other contexts and will not be discussed in detail here. These include: Source Term Code Package (Ref. D.24); CONTAIN (Ref. D.25); MELCOR (Ref. D.26); and MELPROG (Ref. D.27). Other codes were, however, developed or first used for this study. For such codes, various types of quality assurance checks were specifically performed as part of the NUREG-1150 study. The LHS code was reviewed in 1984; a user's manual was written (Ref. D.28) and the code has been released to the National Energy Software Center at Argonne National Laboratory. LHS has been in use at Sandia National Laboratories for several years. Since the draft analyses, the EVNTRE and PSTEVNT codes (Ref. D.29) were subject to line-by-line scrutiny and a series of functional tests. User's manuals were written for these codes, and the codes are being released to the National Energy Software Center. The XSOR codes were subject to a line-by-line review by project staff at the Sandia National Laboratories (SNL) and to an independent validation/verification study done at the Battelle Columbus Division and reported as Reference D.30. The PARTITION code (Ref. D.31) was subject to a functional review by the project staff. Its user's manual will be published in 1989. The RISQUE code was functionally reviewed by the SNL staff and elsewhere (Ref. D.29); a list of this code is included as an appendix to Reference D.32. Benchmarking and verification of the current version of the MACCS code, Version 1.5, is now under way. A review has been performed of the chronic exposure pathway modeling (Ref. D.33).

- **Cross-Plant Reviews:** For the accident progression, source term, and consequence modeling, general consistency in phenomenological assumptions and the level of treatment of severe accident phenomena was achieved across the five-plant analyses. This was accomplished primarily through a series of informal interactions among plant analysts and review of the treatment of specific phenomena by the project leader. For example, the Surry accident progression event tree (APET) was used as a base to build the Zion and Sequoyah APETs. The Grand Gulf and Peach Bottom analysts worked jointly to adapt parts of the Grand Gulf APET to Peach Bottom. The treatment of hydrogen (important to the Sequoyah and Grand Gulf analyses) was derived jointly by the Sequoyah and Grand Gulf analysts.

- **Utility Reviews:** An important element of a risk study of a nuclear power plant is the assurance that the risk model is an accurate and up-to-date representation of that plant. For the four plants in this study for which an essentially new risk analysis was performed (Surry, Sequoyah, Peach Bottom, and Grand Gulf), contact with the appropriate utility was maintained throughout the conduct of the study. For the Zion plant, where the accident frequency analysis was a modification of an existing PRA (Ref. D.34), the analysts met with the utility to discuss plant design and operational changes that had occurred since the performance of that PRA.

The present version of NUREG-1150 will undergo a multifaceted review in the near future. This will be a critical review of all important aspects of the document through a formal peer review, university research, professional society discussions, and a public workshop. The emphasis in these forums will be on the responsiveness of the present version of NUREG-1150 to comments on the draft report as well as on how the technology for assessing risk can be improved.

Comment: The analyses of draft NUREG-1150 are not state of the art. The most advanced theoretical and analytical techniques are not always used. Some data are even outdated while other data are ignored or are inappropriately applied.

Response:

A discussion of the methods that were used in the current version of NUREG-1150 is provided in Appendix A. The broad diversity of experts who interpreted published data for the current analyses ensured that the data were up to date and correctly applied. These data reflect the design and operational status of the five plants as of March 1988.

Comment: There must be a consistent and distinct use of terms such as randomness and uncertainty, frequency and probability. In the draft NUREG-1150 report, terminology is sometimes used loosely.

Response:

The consistency of terminology used in the present version of NUREG-1150 has been improved.

Comment: There is a general disregard for technical rigor in the draft NUREG-1150 risk analyses.

Response:

It appears that such a general conclusion was reached based on specific deficiencies in the draft risk analyses, including the process for obtaining expert judgments, the apparent lack of quality assurance reviews, the use of unreviewed and undocumented computer codes, and the reliance on severe accident information from NRC contractors to a greater extent than on that from other sources. Each of these specific issues is discussed elsewhere in this appendix. The NRC staff and its contractors believe that the present version of NUREG-1150 is based on analyses with appropriate technical rigor.

D.3.4 Other Comments on Methods

Comment: The NUREG-1150 results do not appear to be reproducible. It appears that the results seem dependent on the particular experts whose judgments were factored into the analyses. A different selection of experts would make different judgments that would lead to different risk estimates. This point goes beyond just the subjective judgment of experts and extends into the analytical techniques. If another random number generator were to be used in the sampling scheme for generating uncertainty estimates, different uncertainty bands and hence risk estimates would result.

Response:

The selection of experts will have an effect on the results of the risk analyses discussed in this report, as well as in any other circumstance where expert judgment is used. However, given the necessity of using expert judgment, the formal procedures used for the present version of NUREG-1150 offer the following advantages: the expert panels are established using experts from a wide spectrum of interests, minimizing the potential impact of any one group; the use of judgments is explicitly acknowledged; and the rationales underlying judgments are documented.

With any analysis involving a Monte Carlo process, it is inevitable that the results will vary somewhat, depending on the details of the sampling algorithm and the way it is implemented. The variability associated with the sampling process has been investigated as part of the analysis process and found to be small (Ref. D.32). As discussed in Chapter 2, the reader should recognize that the estimated mean values can vary by no more than a factor of two, depending on the Monte Carlo sample that is used. This variability can also impact the relative contribution of factors (e.g., plant damage state frequencies) to the mean, particularly when there are a small number of contributors.

Comment: The methods used to calculate risk are complex and subjective, which is in part because of the performance of uncertainty analysis. The risk-dominant issues should be quantitatively defined with detailed calculations or experimental evidence.

Response:

The present version of NUREG-1150 has made extensive use of mechanistic computer code calculations and pertinent experimental results available from both NRC-sponsored research and that sponsored by the nuclear industry. However, the spectrum of accident conditions is wide, precluding mechanistic calculations for all conditions. For potentially important uncertainty issues, such as containment loads at vessel breach, expert judgment was obtained for a variety of generalized conditions such as vessel breach at high pressure, intermediate pressure, or low pressure, with a flooded reactor cavity or a dry reactor cavity. Typically, the experts could base their judgments on the results of mechanistic code calculations or experiments of only some of these conditions. Parametric codes were used to predict the source terms for a wide range of sequence variations.

Comment: The practice of evaluating complex physical and chemical phenomena in nuclear reactor accidents is not well conceived. This evaluation should be done using such classical methods as scaling analysis, zeroth order estimates, and ideal model simulations.

Response:

Subsequent to the accident at Three Mile Island on March 28, 1979, the NRC undertook a major research effort to develop an improved understanding of severe accident behavior (Ref. D.35). The focus of this effort has been the development and validation of computer codes that estimate the variety of complex processes that can occur in a severe accident. A two-tiered approach to code development has been followed. At one level, detailed mechanistic codes have been developed that analyze a specific aspect of severe accident behavior, such as the use of the CORCON code to analyze the attack of concrete by hot core debris. The second level involves the development of codes that treat all aspects of a severe accident but in less phenomenological detail. Both of NRC's codes of this type, the Source Term Code Package and MELCOR, were used in the source term estimation in this risk study. In the current version of this study, greater use was made of the detailed mechanistic codes than in the draft report. The general approach to the development of the suite of NRC severe accident codes has been reviewed previously by a number of peer committees and is responsive to the recommendations of the review by the American Physical Society (Ref. D.36). These codes are supported by a range of experiments to obtain fundamental data, separate effects, and integral confirmation.

Comment: Various aspects of the draft risk studies lack consistency within each risk study and among the risk studies leading to an unevenness in the overall approach. The level of detail of modeling in each analysis varies, lacking in some portions and extremely detailed in others. A given technical issue is treated differently at different plants. The analysis of the Zion plant is less detailed than the analysis of the other plants.

Response:

With the exception of the Zion accident frequency analysis, the NUREG-1150 methods have been applied consistently for all five plants. Within a specific plant analysis, issues were treated at varying levels of detail, with additional consideration given to potentially more important issues. This is not an unusual practice in PRAs. Issues common to more than one plant were analyzed using the same methods for each plant. However, the resulting outcome (e.g., the impact on core damage frequency) can vary among plants because of plant design and operational differences.

The Zion accident frequency analysis was indeed different from that performed for the other four plants. This difference is a result of the availability of a relatively recent PRA performed for the utility (Ref. D.34) and extensively reviewed by the NRC staff and its contractors (Ref. D.37). For the present version of NUREG-1150, this PRA (as reviewed) was updated to reflect plant design and operational characteristics as of March 1988. The accident frequency analysis methods in NUREG-1150 used for the Zion plant are discussed in Appendix A, Section A.2.2, to this report.

Comment: Because many aspects of severe accidents cannot be quantified, assumptions are made about the aspects to account for them in the risk calculations. Too often such assumptions lack a firm basis. Furthermore, a given assumption varies from one plant to the next. The assumptions are made conservatively to ensure safety but in doing so make the risk estimates unrealistic. An example is the short battery life assumed in station blackout sequences.

Response:

Efforts were made to make reasonable assumptions in all parts of both the previous draft and the present version of the NUREG-1150 analyses; the bases for the assumptions have been thoroughly documented in the present version of NUREG-1150.

In the analysis of Peach Bottom for draft NUREG-1150, the batteries were assumed to be depleted in 6 hours during a station blackout. The assumption was based on information from the Philadelphia Electric Company (PECo), the utility operating that plant. After additional review by PECo and accounting for operator actions for load shedding, the assumption was changed for the present version of NUREG-1150 to 12 hours. The Grand Gulf analysis also assumed a 12-hour battery life.

Comment: There is a tendency to overemphasize the numerical aspects of probabilistic risk assessment. While the quantitative aspects are important, it is also important as a structured and comprehensive framework for safety analyses.

Response:

The intended uses of NUREG-1150 are discussed in detail in Chapter 13, "NUREG-1150 As a Resource Document." These uses do not focus on the bottom-line quantitative results but on the perspectives gained from the development and application of the complex logic models used to calculate the risk estimates.

D.4 Tracing and Documenting Calculations

D.4.1 Tracing Calculations

Comment: The document is inscrutable. It is nearly impossible to follow the development of the results through the calculations. Intermediate results at key points in the calculations would have been useful in understanding the risk estimates. Some conclusions are unsubstantiated and cannot be traced back to their supporting calculations. Although technical issues are delineated, how they affect the results is not discernible.

Response:

The present version of NUREG-1150 has been extensively restructured, relative to the draft report, to improve its clarity. In particular, the report has been more explicitly described as a summary report, written for people not expert in PRA and, as appropriate, directing the reader to sections of the supporting contractor reports for additional detail.

The risk calculations are very complicated, requiring extensive computer calculations to perform the analyses. Documentation of these analyses is found in supporting contractor reports; this documentation has been restructured to improve the traceability of the work and to expand the discussion of the underlying rationale. An example calculation has been developed for the reader seeking details of the risk analyses, with a description provided of both the individual steps of the risk analysis process and the products of the individual steps. The example calculation is provided in Appendix B.

Comment: Because the sequences are grouped into plant damage states, there is difficulty in connecting what follows core damage with containment failure. This could lead to gaps in the development of specific scenarios and detract from those situations where accident management could be effective.

Response:

PRAs such as those conducted in support of NUREG-1150 consider hundreds of thousands of distinct failure combinations leading to severe accident sequences. It is a practical necessity that grouping of these sequences be performed. Plant damage states have been used in many recent PRAs to accomplish such a grouping.

D.4.2 Completeness of Documentation

Comment: NUREG-1150 represents a large amount of information but many topics are insufficiently discussed, such as descriptions of models, treatment of processes of a severe accident, underlying assumptions, and uses of the risk estimates. The expert judgments and the methods used to obtain those judgments must be fully documented; each judgment should be attributed to the particular expert who gave it, together with the basis and the reasoning for the judgment.

Response:

NUREG-1150 is a summary of large and complex risk studies of five nuclear power plants. All aspects of the study cannot be conveyed in such a summary report. The methods used, supporting rationale, and results are discussed in detail in the set of supporting documents (Refs. D.12 through D.16, D.19 through D.23, D.32, D.38, and D.39). Other supporting information, such as on the principal accident analysis codes used in the study, is described in other available documents.

As discussed in Section D.3.2, the process of obtaining and using expert judgments has been substantially improved for the present version of NUREG-1150. Extensive documentation of the bases for these judgments is a major aspect of the new elicitation process. This documentation is provided in References D.18 and D.39.

D.4.3 Display of Results

Comment: Traditional methods of displaying uncertainty, such as cumulative distribution functions, probability density distributions, best estimates, and central estimates should be provided. The presentation of ranges alone without means or other best estimates tends, as in draft NUREG-1150, to focus excessive attention on the extremes and obscures the advances made in nuclear safety since the Reactor Safety Study.

Response:

The present version of NUREG-1150 uses traditional displays of uncertainty. These displays include probability density functions (approximated by histograms) with mean, median, and 5th and 95th percentile values shown. Complementary cumulative distribution functions are used to convey results of source term and offsite consequence results. Other displays, such as bar charts and pie charts, are used to convey supplemental information.

D.5 Accident Frequency Analysis

D.5.1 Logic

Comment: No thermal-hydraulic analyses were done to define what constitutes a successful operation of a given system. Instead, success and failure were defined from previous studies on other plants.

Response:

Numerous thermal-hydraulic studies were available from which conclusions could be drawn relative to safety systems performance under a range of plant conditions. In addition, information was obtained from knowledgeable personnel at the plant sites to better understand system responses under abnormal conditions and some plant-specific thermal-hydraulic calculations (Refs. D.20 and D.22) using the MELCOR (Ref. D.11) and the LTAS (Ref. D.40) codes. The combination of general analyses and plant-specific information is believed to be adequate to define success criteria.

Comment: Support systems and the activation and control of various systems by other systems were not taken into account in the accident frequency analysis.

Response:

Support systems and their impact on emergency core cooling, containment safeguard systems, and other front-line systems were explicitly considered in both the draft and the present version of NUREG-1150. Detailed system-by-system analyses were performed to determine the potential impact of support systems. Those dependencies that were critical to the functioning of a system were then included in the models.

Actuation and control dependencies between systems were taken into account, although a detailed study of each actuating and control device was not performed. Instead, these dependencies were represented with generic failure rates with significant uncertainty bounds. This approach is considered adequate because such failures have not been found important in reviewing the results of other PRAs.

Comment: Prior PRAs, from which much information was derived, were used even though many changes in plant hardware and operation have occurred since the PRAs were performed that are not reflected by these PRAs.

Response:

Prior PRAs provided a basis from which to start the risk studies. Plant design and operational information, obtained from the individual utilities, was obtained and used to perform the actual risk studies.

Comment: The mathematical treatment of common-cause failure (CCF) is more consistent and detailed than in many previous studies. Nonetheless, the importance of CCF dictates that a more comprehensive and quantitative treatment of the factors affecting it be undertaken. The CCF modeling should be improved as several examples illustrate: For a station blackout, the notion of a CCF of the batteries is difficult to accept because the batteries are monitored, are in use, and are checked daily; for a loss of component cooling water (CCW), the CCF of the CCW pumps is difficult to accept because some pumps are normally operating while others are kept in a standby mode; the fuel supply to diesel generators is not mentioned as a potential CCF, etc. In PRAs, CCF must be modeled realistically.

Response:

The NUREG-1150 study treated common-cause failure in as realistic a way as presently possible. The objective was to estimate risk using the best available information and tools given the limitations of available data.

The analyses reported in the supporting documentation had the following characteristics with respect to CCF:

- System interdependencies were modeled in the fault tree analysis and common-mode failures were included as appropriate.

- Common-mode failures of pumps, valves, batteries, diesel generators, and other hardware were explicitly considered.

- To the extent possible, the current analyses used plant-specific data. However, where the plant-specific information was inadequate to generate new CCF models, such failures were treated with realistic generic models, including recent advances in the methods for creating such models.

- Common-cause failures induced by earthquakes were considered when two plants were analyzed; the external-event analysis examined other potential sources of common-mode failures such as fire.

Nevertheless, it is recognized that there are a number of things that are not done in these analyses. These excluded activities were:

- Unique CCFs that might be postulated as a result of faulty construction or counterfeit parts are not modeled, except as they may appear in the common-cause failure data base.

- Detailed examination of the root causes for CCFs was not made.

- The CCF analysis inherently lacks reliable and identifiable data. Under these circumstances, it is often necessary to rely heavily upon engineering judgment, leading to the possibility for disagreements about the outcomes.

While present CCF models are believed to be reasonable, it is also clear that improvements can be made. To this end, the NRC has ongoing programs for developing improved models for CCF analysis.

Comment: Inappropriate application of models of human reliability focused on procedural errors and resulted in low human error contributions to core melt frequency.

Response:

Human error contributed less to the core melt frequency than expected, but, in most cases, there are reasons for the lower values. These include:

- The low probabilities due to human errors were not necessarily a consequence of a simple analysis. For example, low human error probabilities were produced for the BWR ATWS sequence using an extremely detailed human reliability analysis (Ref. D.41).

- Some small values reflect the availability (at the plant) and consideration (in the analysis) of symptom-based procedures. With such procedures, an operator responds to an accident treating conditions that are indicated on the control panel, such as ensuring that the reactor is tripped, the turbine is tripped, the vital electrical buses are energized, and so on. These conditions are treated without recognizing the sequence. The use of such procedures improves the performance of the operators and likewise reduces human error values.

- In some circumstances, low operator error values are the result of the combination of probabilities for several independent actions. When such circumstances occurred, additional checks were performed to ensure the reasonableness of the results obtained. In the current analyses, all combinations of human errors less than 1E-4 required additional analysis and justification; few of these cases occurred.

D.5.2 Quantification

Comment: Generic failure data are used in the risk studies, yet each study is claimed to be plant specific. Furthermore, generic data are sometimes used even when plant-specific data are available.

Response:

Plant-specific information has been obtained (where available) and used for key systems in each plant. Where such information is inadequate for these key systems and for less important systems, generic data have been employed. As a result there is a mix of information sources underlying the analysis. This is discussed in more detail in Section A.2.1 of Appendix A.

Comment: Calculations by the industry indicate that it is important to thoroughly examine the probability that the automatic depressurization system (ADS) in boiling water reactors would not fail when it is assumed that dc power fails.

Response:

Analysis performed for the boiling water reactors indicated that the ADS is dependent upon dc power in that both the logic for control and the valve power come from dc sources. The logic system is failed if the primary dc supply bus and the switching relay to the backup bus are lost. Two dc buses would have to fail to lose all valve power. Given this dependency, the expected life of batteries in station blackout conditions was an important issue. In the analyses for draft NUREG-1150, effective battery life was estimated to be 6 hours (in station blackout conditions) for the Peach Bottom plant. Based upon reviews and discussions with the Philadelphia Electric Company and accounting for operator load-shedding actions, this battery life was extended to 12 hours for the present risk analysis. A 12-hour battery life was also calculated for the Grand Gulf analysis.

Comment: Confidence limits on the success probabilities assigned to the fault trees appear to be derived from the high and low probabilities of operator action. This is not mathematically correct, and such limits should be viewed only as upper and lower bounds.

Response:

Operator actions were treated the same as all other events in the fault trees. That is, the failure probability of each action was assigned a mean value and a probability distribution. The combination of individual event probabilities was then performed using mathematical sampling techniques, ensuring the appropriate mathematical treatment.

Comment: The analysis of a rupture of a steam generator tube is incorrect because the frequency of a credible tube rupture sequence is multiplied by the probability of auxiliary feedwater system failure, thus lowering the frequency of a legitimate core melt accident sequence by three to four orders of magnitude. There is no reason to believe a value of 9E–9/reactor year when detailed plant-specific PRAs have consistently estimated the frequency in the range of 1.6E–6 to 1.0E–5/reactor year.

Response:

The analysis of steam generator tube rupture frequency and consequences has been substantially modified for the present version of NUREG–1150. Core damage frequencies obtained using the new analyses are consistent with the values cited above as results from other recent PRAs.

Comment: The models of core degradation are unrealistic. Severe fuel damage is defined to cover all cases where fuel cladding is damaged, but cladding integrity is not a measure of fuel damage and results in an overestimate of risk when it is defined as such.

Response:

The models that are used to predict fuel damage do not attempt to describe all the complex phenomena associated with severe core degradation in detail. The thermal-hydraulic model in the Source Term Code Package (STCP) (Ref. D.24) uses simplified models and assumptions for the treatment of some of the very complex steps in the core degradation process, such as fuel slumping into the lower plenum of a reactor vessel. However, the current version of NUREG–1150 did not rely heavily on the thermal-hydraulic model in the STCP for the estimation of the core meltdown process. The results of analysis with the MELCOR code (Ref. D.26), the MELPROG code (Ref. D.27), and the MAAP code (Ref. D.42) assisted project analysts and other experts in estimating the magnitude of parameters directly associated with core melt progression, such as hydrogen production and the mode of reactor vessel failure. Although the MELCOR code and the MELPROG code predict some core meltdown processes in more detail than the models in the STCP, the simplifications in the models of these codes must also be recognized.

In the current version of NUREG–1150, core damage is defined as a significant core uncovery occurrence with reflooding of the core not imminently expected. The result is a prolonged uncovery of the core that leads to damaged fuel and an expected release of fission products from the fuel.

The current version of NUREG–1150 treats the recovery of core with fuel damage differently from earlier probabilistic risk analyses. Under a broad range of conditions, given that a water supply is recovered prior to vessel failure, the likelihood of recovering a core and arresting an accident was evaluated. Based largely on the experience of the accident at Three Mile Island Unit 2, debris bed coolability analyses, and supplemental calculations of head failure, the likelihood of arresting further core damage decreased as the fraction of the fuel relocated to the bottom head at the time of coolant recovery increased.

D.6 Containment Loads and Structural Response

D.6.1 Accident Progression Event Tree: Logic

Comment: The large amount of detail in the accident progression event trees (APETs) gives the impression that more is known about containment events and phenomena than is actually known. It is difficult to believe the results of a complex tree that yields a tremendous number of pathways that are then aggregated into a dozen or so groups. Not only does a complex tree give a false impression but it limits any review of how the tree was constructed.

Response:

The rationale for developing a detailed APET is to provide an explicit treatment of all phenomena that can have a significant impact on the accident progression and the magnitude of the fission product source terms. Even if the existing capability to predict some of these phenomena is limited, it is important that the phenomena be recognized, at least for characterizing the uncertainty in the results.

The size of an APET does not affect the clarity of the results. Pathways with similar characteristics can be grouped to form simpler event trees as has been done to present results in the current version of the main report.

A detailed review of the APETs is difficult but not impossible. In the current documentation, the APETs were sufficiently described. Reviews were performed as described in Section D.3.3.

Comment: Early containment failure calculations are based on flawed accident progression event trees. Pathways with a potential for pressure reduction in the reactor coolant system are neglected.

Response:

In the draft analyses, the PWR event trees included several important depressurization mechanisms, namely, induced reactor coolant system hot leg failure, induced steam generator tube rupture, and reactor coolant pump seal failure. The BWR event trees took into account the operation of the automatic depressurization systems. In the current analyses, the PWR event trees have been revised to include a possible reactor coolant primary system and/or secondary system depressurization by the operators and by power-operated relief valves (PORVs) sticking open. The combined effect of these depressurization mechanisms was found to be important in the present risk analysis.

Comment: The risk reduction due to containment venting can be assessed only after a detailed study of venting procedures, relevant hardware, and plant response has been done. There is much disagreement as to the scenarios leading up to venting, the manner in which to vent, the vent size, re-isolating, and the effectiveness of venting. Containment venting should be included in the analyses only if procedures and equipment exist at the given plant.

Response:

The actions included in the NUREG-1150 analyses that could result in deliberate containment venting were those permitted by plant-specific operational procedures. Of the five plants studied, only two (Peach Bottom and Grand Gulf) had such procedures. For these two, the probability of successful venting was a function of the available procedures and hardware. For the Peach Bottom plant, it was found that venting with existing hardware and procedures was viable (had a high probability of success) for one type of accident, the long-term loss of decay heat removal. For other sequences, the probability of successful venting was of low probability, principally because of hardware limitations (Ref. D.43). For the Grand Gulf plant, the situation is similar. For the long-term loss of decay heat removal sequences, the procedures exist and operators can vent from the control room. Credit was not given in the most frequent accident sequences (i.e., station blackouts) because of unavailability of needed dc power.

D.6.2 Containment Loading Phenomena

Comment: Studies of severe accident phenomena are conflicting. Some studies predict global hydrogen burns while others conclude that global combustion cannot occur. Some studies show that hydrogen detonations can occur while others show that diffusive burning will occur. Some studies show early containment failure while other studies show that an early failure can occur only as an interfacing-system loss-of-coolant accident. Some studies suggest that the steel shell of a containment can be breached when contacted by molten core debris while other studies suggest that heat will be conducted away from the shell at a sufficient rate to prevent meltthrough. The conflicting studies give little confidence in the conclusions that are drawn from them.

Response:

It is agreed that the present information base on severe reactor accident phenomenology is limited and that this base sometimes contains conflicting data. The state of this information base is one reason why the NRC staff chose to characterize individual phenomenological issues and the associated risk analyses by probability distributions, rather than single-valued estimates, and make use of expert judgment, as done in other analyses of poorly understood issues, to review and interpret the available information.

Comment: NUREG-1150 states that for BWRs direct containment heating is not a prominent cause of containment failure because the core support design will allow limited portions of the core to melt and fall into the lower vessel head, causing localized vessel failure before the bulk of the core accumulates in the lower head. This is assumed; no calculations or experiments are offered in support of this hypothesis.

Response:

Many of the values used in the analyses found in draft NUREG–1150 were inadequately justified. The current analyses have been more thoroughly documented. Issues such as the loads on a containment building at the time of reactor vessel breach, including the effects of direct containment heating, were determined through expert interpretation of available calculations and experiments. Details of these analyses are discussed in References D.18 and D.39.

Comment: There are large uncertainties associated with direct containment heating (DCH). An industry group studied DCH and found it not to be a contributor to containment failure in the Sequoyah cavity design. Small-scale experiments indicate that 90 percent of the ejected melt will remain inside the cavity. It is thought that, in the PWR reactor coolant system (RCS), hot leg failure can occur prior to the bottom head failure, precluding direct containment heating because the RCS would be at low pressure at the time of vessel failure. But other experimental studies done at a national laboratory indicate that DCH can occur. Analytical studies suggest that assuming depressurization by operators will not alleviate the problem since there are some accident scenarios in which depressurization cannot be achieved because of a lack of dc power.

Response:

Since draft NUREG–1150 was published in February 1987, the information base for quantifying important issues has been expanded. Among those that received considerable attention were contributors to containment loads during high-pressure melt ejection (including direct containment heating) and the potential for depressurizing the reactor vessel (including RCS hot leg failure). However, the information base remains incomplete. In the present study, experts in severe accidents were asked to interpret the information base and to generate probability distributions required for risk analyses. The experts who participated in this assessment and the information used to quantify containment loads at vessel breach are discussed in Sections C.5 and C.6 of Appendix C.

Through expert judgment, it was concluded that the upper end of the range of potential containment loads accompanying high-pressure melt ejection reached high values (i.e., several times the containment design pressures). A containment analysis indicated, with relatively high confidence, that the Surry and the Zion containment structures could accommodate all but the highest of these loads. A similar conclusion could be drawn for the Sequoyah containment only if certain containment safety features operate (e.g., a substantial inventory of ice is in the ice condenser at the time of vessel breach). Regarding the RCS pressure at vessel breach, the current analyses indicate that in the majority of station blackout accident scenarios, at least one of several mechanisms (e.g., temperature-induced hot leg failure, reactor coolant pump seal failures) will reduce the pressure in the reactor coolant system to sufficiently low values to make high-pressure melt ejection unlikely. During other types of severe accident scenarios, manual actions, such as opening the pressurizer PORV, are likely to occur to similarly reduce the likelihood of high-pressure melt ejection.

Comment: When the necessary conditions exist, steam explosions can occur in a reactor vessel as a result of a degraded core contacting water in the lower head, and the explosion can be sufficiently energetic to cause reactor coolant system and containment building failure. Because of large uncertainties in this technical issue, it should be mathematically treated as a full issue in and of itself and not part of some other issue. The treatment should be consistent with previous studies done by the NRC and the industry.

Response:

The probability of steam explosions sufficient to fail the containment building was treated as a separate issue and a probability distribution developed for the present version of NUREG–1150. This distribution was developed by the NUREG–1150 project staff using, as an initial basis, the work of the Steam Explosion Review Group (Ref. D.44). This work was updated (incorporating the possible effect of new information) by polling the individual members of the review group.

Comment: NUREG–1150 continues to carry the steam explosion issue along even though all but a few steam explosion researchers concluded that no issue remains. Considering this issue as a mechanism for reactor vessel and containment failure is inconsistent with a previous study done by the NRC (the Steam Explosion Review Group).

Response:

As discussed in the previous response, the present NUREG–1150 analyses of the potential for containment building failure by in-vessel steam explosions are based on the work of the Steam Explosion Review Group.

Comment: In draft NUREG–1150, there is an accident sequence in which a containment failure leads to a failure of emergency core cooling, leading to core meltdown. This does not seem plausible.

Response:

This type of accident sequence was first identified in the Reactor Safety Study (Ref. D.7) in 1975 as the S2C accident sequence in the Surry plant and as the TW sequence in the Peach Bottom plant. Since that time, analyses have been performed that indicate that the S2C sequence would not result in core damage in the Surry plant. However, the TW sequence has been investigated in a number of boiling water reactor PRAs and found in some cases to have a not insignificant frequency. For the present study of the Peach Bottom plant, this accident sequence made a small contribution to the core melt frequency, principally because the progression of the accident was slow, permitting operator intervention to preclude core damage.

Comment: The major contributors to Peach Bottom containment building failure appear to be the assumed overpressure failure in the wetwell above the water line, drywell head failure, or the assumed meltthrough of the drywell shell. None of these failure modes are supported to the degree necessary to warrant the level of confidence in the central estimate.

Response:

Consideration of these failure modes in the present version of NUREG–1150 made use of a spectrum of experimental and calculated data. Because these data were often conflicting, expert judgment was used to interpret the data and to develop the probability distributions needed for the risk studies.

The results of the Peach Bottom risk analysis for the present version of NUREG–1150 indicate that meltthrough of the drywell shell is the principal cause of early containment failure in that plant. However, high-pressure melt ejection remains a significant contributor to early containment failure.

Comment: The probabilities of hydrogen detonation in the BWR Mark III containment building and hydrogen combustion-induced failure of the Sequoyah containment building are overestimated. A detonation requires a very high concentration or a geometric configuration that will produce a sufficient flame acceleration. Data from over 40 tests in the Hydrogen Control Owners' Group 1/4-Scale Test Facility and other test data support the notion of containment-wide mixing that precludes high local concentrations and thus local detonations. The effects of diffusive combustion at the suppression pool surface controls the global hydrogen concentration from 4 to 6 volume percent, precluding flame acceleration. In a study of Sequoyah by an industry group, calculations indicate that during a station blackout accident, natural circulation in the containment will permit the recombination of combustible gases as the gases pass over hot debris in a reactor cavity without placing severe loads on the containment. The large hydrogen loads that have been calculated result from inadequate credit given to the recombination of combustible gases.

Response:

Experts, listed in Section C.4, of Appendix C, were asked to interpret information on hydrogen combustion. Each expert was familiar with published data and analyses regarding hydrogen combustion phenomena and their applicability to the distribution of hydrogen in a containment building, the ignition of hydrogen, and the attendant loads. Using these data, they developed distributions characterizing their estimate of and uncertainty in selected parameters, such as ignition frequency, probability of deflagration/ detonation transition, and combustion loads. A summary of the probability distributions and their application in the Grand Gulf and the Sequoyah risk analyses is provided in Section C.4 of Appendix C.

Comment: The initiation of containment sprays in a BWR Mark III containment building should not lead to significant de-inerting. As the sprays cool the containment atmosphere, the reducing pressure will allow the suppression pool to flash as the saturation temperature is reached. The flashing will produce steam and at least partially re-inert the containment atmosphere. It is believed that a hydrogen burn after re-inerting is insufficiently energetic to cause containment building failure.

Response:

The recovery of ac power allows both the containment sprays and the residual heat removal (RHR) system to operate. Eventually, the suppression pool will be cooled by the RHR system; this precludes flashing, and, hence, the containment will de-inert. It is thought that in a containment previously inerted by steam, and after the recovery of both ac power and containment sprays, the severity of a hydrogen burn depends on the relative timing of ignition. Ignition well after recovery of ac power (when the containment atmosphere is not inert) could result in a severe hydrogen burn. However, if ignition occurs soon after ac power recovery, a slow incomplete burn that does not threaten the containment or the drywell could occur. Such incomplete burns are considered in the accident progression trees for Grand Gulf.

The spray de-inerting scenario is not as important in the current analyses as it was in the analyses of the earlier draft of NUREG-1150. Previously, the core damage frequency was dominated by long-term station blackout scenarios when the containment atmosphere is inert at the time of reactor vessel breach. Currently, it is dominated by short-term station blackouts when the containment atmosphere is not inert at the time of vessel breach.

Comment: The phenomena in core-concrete interactions are not well understood; the models used are only approximations that are inadequately validated. But even if detailed models could be formulated, it is unnecessary to be concerned with such details while neglecting to examine the location and the behavior of previously evolved fission products. Because a molten core has lost nearly all its fission product gases, the core-concrete interaction is depleted of fission products.

Response:

The major phenomena of a core-concrete interaction are reasonably well known and understood. Based on experimental studies, models have been developed that adequately represent the phenomena (Refs. D.24 and D.45 through D.47).

While a molten core has lost essentially all the volatile fission products by the time it has penetrated the reactor vessel and begun to interact with concrete, it will still retain a majority of the nonvolatile species. The subsequent evolution of these nonvolatile species can have a significant impact on the overall consequences.

D.6.3 Containment Structural Response

Comment: There is no universal definition of what constitutes a containment failure, including leak failures and penetration failures.

Response:

The accident progression event trees make a distinction between different failure locations and magnitudes of leakage. The source terms for each accident progression bin account for the effects of these differences in leakage behavior. The issue of location and mode of failure is probably treated in greater detail in this study than in any previous PRA, making use of available calculations and experimental data on containment building responses to severe accident loads.

Comment: Experimental data on the ultimate potential strength of containment buildings and their failure modes are lacking. This lack of data renders questionable the methods used in draft NUREG–1150 for assigning probabilities and locations of failures.

Response:

The present data on the potential strength of containment structures under severe accident loadings and the potential modes of failure are limited. For the current analyses, the structural engineering experts who reviewed and interpreted the available information are listed in Section C.8 of Appendix C.

Except for the Grand Gulf plant, the experts addressed the response of the containment buildings studied in NUREG–1150 to a range of quasistatic pressure loads associated with severe accident conditions. Other containment failure mechanisms, such as penetration by a missile, structural failure due to impulse loads (e.g., hydrogen detonation for Grand Gulf and Sequoyah), and meltthrough by molten material, were not addressed by structural experts directly but were addressed for some plants through other aspects of the risk analysis. For example, drywell shell meltthrough in the Peach Bottom reactor (BWR Mark I containment) was addressed by a separate expert panel.

The results of the experts' reviews and judgments are described in Appendix C of NUREG–1150. Briefly, the median failure pressure ranged from 50 and 65 psig for Grand Gulf and Sequoyah, respectively, to 125 and 130 psig for Surry and Zion, respectively. The uncertainty in these estimates spanned a range of approximately 50 to 70 psi, regardless of the absolute range of the design or failure pressure. For the two large, dry containments, Surry and Zion, the median failure pressure corresponds to approximately three times the containment design pressure. The median failure pressure of 65 psig for the ice condenser containment, Sequoyah, was substantially lower than that for the large, dry containments; however, this value corresponds to more than six times the design pressure. For the two BWR containments, the Mark I at Peach Bottom and the Mark III at Grand Gulf, the ultimate capacity of the containments was estimated to be 150 psig and 50 psig, respectively. This corresponds to approximately three times the respective design pressures. The failure pressure of the Mark I containment was judged to be extremely sensitive to the drywell atmospheric temperature. As described in Appendix C, Section C.8, the ultimate capacity of the Peach Bottom drywell shell may decrease to levels at or below the containment design pressure if the drywell temperature exceeds 1200°F.

Comment: The Electric Power Research Institute (EPRI) has been conducting experiments to confirm the hypothesis that steel-lined concrete containments will develop small leaks before experiencing gross failure when subjected to high internal pressures. Industry computer programs have been modified to represent the behavior of steel liners and concrete. Codes have been developed that have been validated against experiments and can be used to analyze actual containments. This source of information should be used in NUREG–1150.

Response:

Results of the EPRI tests were discussed in the expert elicitation process and were used in quantifying the failure pressure and modes of the concrete containments. A participant in the EPRI program served on the containment performance panel of experts.

Comment: In BWR analyses, secondary containments should be taken into account because there are divergent views on the capability of this structure to withstand a failure of the primary containment and to retain aerosols.

Response:

In the current version of NUREG–1150, the decontamination factor (DF) of the reactor building was quantified through expert interpretation of available data. The judgments on the DFs (for several release rates, steam concentrations, and flow patterns) were based on models of and calculations from mechanistic codes, personally developed models, and experiments. A DF was not applied to the reactor building of the Grand Gulf plant because the most likely failure location is at the top of the containment;

the only structure between the anticipated failure location and the environment is a corrugated metal structure that is judged to fail immediately after containment failure.

Comment: The Peach Bottom analysis was based on the concept of a freestanding structure. However, the failure pressure would be higher than considered in draft NUREG-1150 because the steel shell would get support from the concrete as it expands under pressure loading.

Response:

The performance of the Peach Bottom steel shell was reviewed by an expert panel of structural engineers. Data available to the panel members included an analysis by the Chicago Bridge and Iron Company on the structural capability of the Peach Bottom steel shell, explicitly including the effects of the concrete biological shield surrounding the shell. The results of the expert review are discussed in Section C.8 of Appendix C.

Comment: The assumption that the drywell shell fails as the molten core material contacts the shell is driven by expert judgment. The failure might be delayed or averted if the shell conducts heat away from the contact point rapidly.

Response:

The potential for drywell shell failure by direct contact of molten core material has been analyzed by a number of organizations, including Brookhaven National Laboratory, Oak Ridge National Laboratory, Sandia National Laboratories, Massachusetts Institute of Technology, University of Wisconsin, Fauske & Associates, Inc., and the Electric Power Research Institute. The results of these analyses are conflicting.

For the present version of NUREG-1150, the analyses were reviewed by experts listed in Section C.7 of Appendix C; their results are presented in the same section.

D.7 Source Terms and Consequences

D.7.1 Methods

Comment: The NUREG-1150 study and the findings are inconsistent with past research trends, which have been toward more mechanistic codes resulting in smaller uncertainties. The computer codes used in NUREG-1150 are becoming less mechanistic and the uncertainties appear to be increasing.

Response:

The NUREG-1150 study used a simplified approach for calculating radioactive releases because the large number of such estimates needed to express uncertainty could not all be made with the long-running and resource-intense codes such as the Source Term Code Package (STCP). Simple algorithms were used to make these calculations; the algorithms are collectively known as the XSOR codes. However, the bases for these algorithms were calculations with a set of more mechanistic codes, including the STCP (Ref. D.24), CONTAIN (Ref. D.25), MELCOR (Ref. D.26), and MELPROG (Ref. D.27).

In order to address the adequacy of the estimates provided by the parametric computer codes, complementary calculations were performed with the STCP to benchmark the parametric analyses. In general, the parametric calculations were found to be in reasonable agreement with the calculations from the STCP. Discrepancies in the parametric calculations, relative to the STCP calculations and to expert judgment, could be explained. Details of these comparisons are reported in Reference D.30.

Comment: The uncertainties in risk have not been properly quantified because the Source Term Code Package used in NUREG-1150 does not account for reevolution or resuspension of deposited fission products either in the reactor coolant system following vessel failure or in the containment. High temperatures would cause ruthenium, which is normally nonvolatile, to form oxides, which are volatile.

Response:

The XSOR analyses in both the draft and the present studies account for a number of processes such as revaporization of material deposited on reactor coolant system surfaces and the volatilization of iodine from water pools late in the accident. The characterization of these processes was made in terms of probability distributions from expert elicitations. The bases for the expert judgments were provided by direct experimental evidence and analyses using mechanistic computer codes such as TRENDS (Ref. D.48), which predicts iodine transport in containment, and a revaporization model developed by the Sandia National Laboratories for the SCDAP/RELAP code (Ref. D.49).

The basis for the STCP analysis of the ruthenium release is the CORSOR model, which is a semiempirical model based on a number of reasonably prototypic experiments. The distribution of release estimates that was actually used in the risk study was obtained from a panel of source term experts. The range of release for the ruthenium group is quite broad. The thermodynamics of ruthenium are considered explicitly in the VANESA model in the STCP, which predicts core-concrete release. Vapor species considered by VANESA are Ru, RuO, RuO_2, RuO_3, and RuO_4. Ruthenium oxidation was also considered in the development of source terms for direct containment heating and steam explosions.

Comment: All research efforts in the past several years have been geared toward making the source term estimates more mechanistic. The NUREG-1150 study goes against these trends by developing and using simple algorithms to estimate source terms. The algorithms do not represent the same level of understanding of source terms as do the mechanistic codes, such as the Source Term Code Package (STCP). The algorithms are merely linear combinations of aggregated variables representing many factors determining source terms, one of the most important of which, timing, is not included. At least the important source terms should be calculated with the STCP, not extrapolated with simple parametric codes. There is no justification for assuming that the variables are linearly related as was done in the simplified parametric source term codes.

Response:

With the introduction of quantitative uncertainty analyses in NUREG-1150, a large number of source term calculations became necessary. The number needed was far too many to be performed with a mechanistic code. In addition, no one code contained the "best" models for all phenomena considered potentially important to the transport analyses. As a result, parametric computer codes were developed, based on the results of detailed calculations of accidents by a number of computer codes, including the Source Term Code Package (STCP) (Ref. D.24), the CONTAIN code (Ref. D.25), and other codes.

While time is not a formal variable in the parametric codes, time dependency of fission product release is included, in that the releases are broken up into in-vessel and ex-vessel portions. Other factors include the timing of containment failure, the time periods over which the containment sprays operate, and the timing of concrete attack.

Comment: The NRC must convince the public and the nuclear community that the Source Term Code Package (STCP) is reliable. The STCP imposes choices on model selection, and no attempt has been made to determine if a different choice would give a significantly different outcome. The NRC should hold a workshop on the STCP and publish a description of the STCP. Because the STCP has not been extensively used in the nuclear community, it is important to review the code; an international consensus may be needed.

Response:

The STCP has been extensively reviewed, as discussed in Reference D.24. In that study, the NRC staff assessed the technology for estimating source terms. The study was reviewed by the American Physical Society (reported as Ref. D.36). The STCP and the results obtained with it were an integral part of a series of meetings between the NRC and an industry group (IDCOR) to exchange technical information. In addition, the STCP has also been the subject of validation and verification efforts by groups other than those involved in its development (Refs. D.50 and D.51). It has been used by numerous organizations in the United States and abroad and, through agreements with the NRC, researchers report their experience in using the code.

The default model selections in the STCP are those that are believed to be most consistent with the understanding of relevant phenomena and considering the limitations of the code. A different choice of models yields different results and, for this reason, choices other than default choices are discouraged. Because the modeling of particular scenarios may require use of alternative assumptions, the model choices are still available in the STCP.

The input decks to operate the STCP were developed using the Final Safety Analysis Report of a plant, information from the plant owners, information from the reactor manufacturers, and information obtained during visits to plants. For any particular STCP calculation, the input data were verified.

The NRC staff recognizes that the STCP has limitations, which are reported in Reference D.24. To compensate for the limitation in the NUREG–1150 study, expert judgment was used. The judgment is based on the information available at the time of the calculations, such as experimental studies and analytical studies using the STCP and other codes. The judgments were factored into the risk estimates through empirically based algorithms collectively known as the XSOR codes; the variables in these codes are more general and subjective than the variables found in the mechanistic codes such as the STCP but semiquantitatively account for phenomena for which rigorous models do not exist. Whenever possible, a mechanistic source term calculation benchmarks the XSOR estimates. A study that compares expert opinion, STCP calculations, and XSOR estimates is reported as Reference D.30.

Comment: Natural circulation is a complex phenomenon. There is no evidence in NUREG–1150 to suggest that the complexity is appreciated or that it is adequately modeled.

Response:

The effect of natural circulation in the reactor coolant system on the potential for early failure and depressurization prior to meltthrough of the vessel was an issue considered by one of the expert panels in the current version of NUREG–1150. The panel had access to the results of a number of analyses performed with industry and NRC computer codes, as well as experimental data (Ref. D.18). The likelihood of vessel meltthrough with the reactor coolant system at high pressure is low in the current analyses, in part because of this potential for early depressurization. The possibility of containment bypass resulting from temperature-induced failure of steam generator tubes is also represented in the current analyses. However, the likelihood of this bypass mechanism is assessed to be small.

Natural circulation patterns can also affect the progression of a core meltdown and the production of hydrogen in a reactor vessel. This was taken into account in the current NUREG–1150 analyses; experts interpreted the results of analyses performed with NRC-sponsored codes and also with codes sponsored by the industry.

D.7.2 Supporting Data Base and Modeling Assumptions

Comment: Evidence suggests that cesium iodide is stable but in NUREG–1150 it is modeled otherwise. No data or experience suggest that iodine will revolatilize from a basic aqueous solution that would form because of the high percentage of cesium in fission product releases. Iodine remained in solution in the Three Mile Island plant for several years after the accident.

Response:

Cesium iodide is not completely stable either in transport through the reactor coolant system or in solution. The issue is how much of the more volatile form is produced. Recent experimental evidence and analysis indicate that the production of volatile forms in the reactor coolant system is smaller than characterized in the previous draft of NUREG–1150. The late release of iodine from the suppression pool is an issue that was addressed by an expert review panel for the current version of NUREG–1150. Results of TRENDS code analyses and direct experimental data were considered by the expert panel. The projected pH of the pool was an important consideration. The extent of reevolution obtained in the current study is not as great as in the draft report. For a subcooled suppression pool, the upper bound of the distribution used is 10 percent and the median value is 0.1 percent. For a saturated or boiling suppression pool, larger releases are predicted.

Comment: Key issues that lead to high source terms, such as drywell liner meltthrough, core melt progression, and late iodine release, should be subject to further experimental evaluation.

Response:

Significant research results have been obtained in each of these areas subsequent to the release of draft NUREG-1150. At the time this response is being written, the NRC is in the process of reorganizing and reprioritizing its Severe Accident Research Program, in part to account for insights generated in this study. It is anticipated that the highest priority for research over the next few years will be given to resolving issues associated with potential threats to containment integrity, such as drywell shell meltthrough, rather than to source term phenomenological issues, such as the late release of iodine from water pools.

Comment: Severe fuel damage (SFD) scoping tests on decladded fuel collapse are inappropriate for validating the models of core melt phenomena because the conditions for the experiments and the conditions represented in the codes are different.

Response:

The performance of integral fuel damage experiments always involves substantial compromise in achieving prototypic severe accident conditions. A considerable effort has recently been initiated at the Brookhaven National Laboratory to provide a quantification of scale distortion and the effects associated with extrapolations, correlations, or models used beyond their data base to quantify code uncertainties.

Comment: Steam generator tube rupture occurring as a result of a core damage accident was found to be an important contributor to the probability of containment bypass. This assumes that fission products get into the steam generator; detailed analyses indicate that fission products will deposit in the pressurizer and pressurizer surge line, not in the steam generator. Industry studies suggest otherwise.

Response:

It is not necessary for fission products to deposit in the steam generator to obtain overheating and failure of the tubes. The Westinghouse experiments on natural circulation indicate that the convective flow path can occur to the steam generators by means of stratified flow in the hot legs. Failure of steam generator tubes prior to hot leg or surge line failure is not considered likely. In part because steam generator tubes may be degraded, some likelihood of tube failure was assessed (by an expert panel) and is included in the analyses.

Comment: Many assumptions are made in the modeling of core degradation phenomena, such as 50 percent of a core becoming molten before slumping occurs and a single well-defined melting point. These assumptions have a large effect on the predicted source terms.

Response:

There are some simplifications in the core meltdown models in the Source Term Code Package (STCP), such as the use of a single temperature for fuel melting, which can affect the magnitude of the source term. Of greater significance is the lack of models in the STCP to predict some highly uncertain processes, such as revaporization of fission products from reactor coolant system surfaces after vessel failure. It is important to understand the relationship among the STCP, the XSOR codes, the detailed mechanistic codes, and the use of expert judgment in treating uncertainties in this study. The STCP was only used as a benchmark for the XSOR codes. It played a very small role in the quantification of the accident progression event trees. Probability distributions for the most important uncertain parameters affecting the source terms were determined by expert panels, based in large part on the results of mechanistic code analyses and experimental results. The source term ranges obtained in this study are dominated by the treatment of these uncertain parameters, not by modeling approximations of core melt progression in the STCP.

Comment: Debris cooling is assigned a low likelihood of occurrence in cases where models based on experiments would predict a coolable geometry.

Response:

In the present version, debris coolability was considered for conditions involving water and debris interactions both in-vessel and ex-vessel. Based in part on the experience from the accident at Three Mile Island on March 28, 1979, it was assumed that water recovery of a damaged core in-vessel could result in arresting core degradation. The likelihood of arrest was decreased as a function of the time into the accident. A window of time for recovery was estimated that was determined by the amount of core debris estimated to be on the lower head of the vessel. For minimal core degradation, a high likelihood (0.9) of arrest is assumed if an emergency coolant supply is reestablished. Beyond a level of debris accumulation, the likelihood of arrest is assumed to be low (0.1). The likelihood of arrest decreases linearly over the time interval.

The likelihood of a coolable debris bed being established ex-vessel was assessed for a variety of different conditions that depended on whether the reactor vessel was at high or low pressure at the time of vessel failure, the size of the failure, the depth of the water in the reactor cavity, and the temperature of the debris. For the different cases, the likelihood of the debris bed being coolable ranges from 20 to 90 percent. Of course, a continuous water supply is a prerequisite to long-term coolability.

Comment: Water in the lower head or water injected into the reactor vessel can have a significant effect on accident progression. The possibility that debris can become critical when flooded is never considered.

Response:

In the PWRs, emergency coolant water is borated. The likelihood of recriticality following flooding is considered small and was not represented in this study. In some BWR sequences, a period of time exists when the control blades may have melted and relocated while the fuel pellets are essentially in their normal configuration. Under these circumstances, reflooding could result in a critical condition. In the present study, the likelihood of recriticality under these specific conditions was considered high but the possibility of an energetic excursion with the potential to fail the vessel was assessed to be small (Ref. D.18).

Comment: In the Sequoyah analysis, it is recognized that water can boil away from debris in a reactor cavity leading to a core-concrete interaction after the ice is depleted and the containment has failed. The scenario does not seem correct because the steam should condense and replenish the debris bed with coolant.

Response:

The analyses account for condensation in the containment and the replenishment of water in the reactor cavity. Dryout of the debris bed only occurs after containment failure and an extended period of steam loss from the containment.

Comment: Data from the accident at Three Mile Island do not support the core melt and fission product release models.

Response:

To the extent that TMI-2 data can be interpreted to evaluate the magnitude of fission product release and the extent of fuel damage during core uncovery, the TMI-2 data are consistent with the Source Term Code Package (STCP) analyses. Benchmark analysis with the STCP shows good agreement with the pressure history (Ref. D.52). Examination of TMI-2 core debris indicates that 70 to 80 percent of the iodine and cesium had escaped the core debris, much of which had never been completely melted (Ref. D.53). These results are consistent with the STCP analyses. Because of the subsequent flooding of the TMI-2 vessel, the examination of the reactor coolant system samples was not able to provide information on the extent of radionuclide deposition during the period of core uncovery and fission product release from the fuel.

Comment: In the risk study, an assumption was made that 5 percent of a population surrounding a nuclear power plant will not evacuate during a severe accident. No basis for this assumption was given. Actual emergency events, both with and without emergency plans, should be used to develop a well-founded value. The assumption should take into account a failure in offsite emergency response, such as may be caused by the failure of buildings, roads, and bridges during an earthquake. A realistic assumption must be used because it significantly affects the calculated consequences.

Response:

The assumed 5 percent non-evacuation of the population within the 10-mile emergency planning zone (EPZ) of a reactor that was used in the calculations for draft NUREG-1150 is conservative. In the current study, the assumption was changed to 0.5 percent, based on the following rationale. The plants that were studied in NUREG-1150 have detailed and well-maintained emergency plans, which also have provisions for evacuating from special facilities within the EPZ. Because an evacuation is preplanned, it is expected to be nearly complete. The preplanned evacuation should be distinguished from unplanned and impromptu evacuations prompted by transportation accidents involving toxic chemicals, accidents at chemical plants, or natural disasters. The specific value used (0.5 percent) was derived from an actual use of a nuclear emergency plan (for a nearby chemical accident). The current study includes displays of the offsite consequences and risk with assumptions on the alternative modes of emergency response within the EPZ, such as evacuation, early relocation, sheltering, and partial (i.e., 0 to 5 miles) evacuation/partial (i.e., 5 to 10 miles) sheltering. Sensitivity calculations of severe accident consequences during an earthquake, assuming a degraded emergency response, are reported in the supplements of NUREG-1150 (Refs. D.12 and D.13).

Comment: It is unreasonable to assume that, once an individual evacuates beyond 15 miles from a damaged reactor, no further dose is received.

Response:

In the current consequence analysis, an individual is assumed to avoid further radiation exposures after reaching a radial distance of 20 miles from a reactor. People who evacuated from the 10-mile emergency planning zone (EPZ) of the Grand Gulf and Peach Bottom plants would need about 3 to 4 hours to travel to a distance of 20 miles from these reactors; people who evacuated from the 10-mile EPZ of the Surry, Sequoyah, and Zion plants would need about 7 to 11 hours to travel to a distance of 20 miles from those reactors. It seems reasonable to assume that by then the location of the radioactive plume and the area contaminated by it would have been known and people would have been advised on how to avoid it.

Comment: The MACCS code should be thoroughly documented and benchmarked. A study should be done of how the MACCS code compares to other codes. The MACCS code should be thoroughly verified and validated to ensure the validity and accuracy of the models, data, and assumptions.

Response:

In late 1987 the NRC staff began an inhouse benchmarking activity on the version of the MACCS code (Version 1.4) used for draft NUREG-1150. This activity consisted of a comparison of MACCS 1.4 results with the results from various research groups calculating consequences using their own consequence codes. The research groups were members of the Organisation for Economic Co-operation and Development/Nuclear Energy Agency/Committee on Safety of Nuclear Installations (OECD/NEA/CSNI). The benchmarking activity revealed errors in MACCS 1.4 and these are reported in References D.54 and D.55.

A comparative review has been performed at the Institute for Energy Technology, Norway, of the chronic exposure pathways modeled in MACCS 1.5 with other consequence codes used by the OECD member countries. The findings are reported as Reference D.33.

The Idaho National Engineering Laboratory (INEL) performed the quality assurance and verification of MACCS 1.5. Sandia National Laboratories (SNL), the developers of the code, assisted INEL because the code had not been adequately documented. The quality assurance program was a line-by-line check of the Fortran coding and crosschecking with the model equations for consistency.

Corrections of most of the errors identified in the Norwegian and INEL reviews were completed in MACCS 1.5 used in this version of NUREG–1150. The residual errors in the MACCS code appear to cause an error of about a factor of two in the latent cancer fatality and population dose estimates; the errors in the code will be corrected before the code is made available to the public. The documentation (user's manual, model descriptions, and programmer's manual), the Norwegian review, and a report of the final crosschecking by INEL (Ref. D.56) are expected to be completed in the summer of 1989.

Comment: It seems to be surprising and erroneous that the bulk of the late fatalities associated with large radionuclide releases is derived from the long-term doses committed via food chain pathways of exposure at low levels of individual dose. It contradicts the results of earlier studies (such as the Reactor Safety Study (Ref. D.7), the German Risk study (Ref. D.57), and the Sizewell B calculations (Ref. D.58)), which concluded that the bulk of the late fatalities is associated with relatively high levels of individual dose attributable to relatively short-term exposure following an accident. Substantial work is required to verify this important difference.

Response:

Errors were found in the calculations of the radiological consequences from the food chain pathways of exposure. These errors were partly from errors in the input to the consequence analysis code, MACCS 1.4, and partly from incorrect modeling of the removal of cesium from the root zone. The incorrect modeling assumed little removal of cesium from the root zone because of irreversible binding of cesium to the soil or cesium percolating through the soil beyond the root zone. This caused the root uptake pathway ingestion doses to be unreasonably large.

D.7.3 Comparisons with Accident at Chernobyl

Comment: Offsite doses (versus distances) reported in NUREG–1150 for some of the source terms are too high and indicate a potential for causing prompt fatalities in the offsite population. In contrast, there were no prompt fatalities outside the plant in the Chernobyl accident.

Response:

The potential of a large radioactive release to the atmosphere to result in high doses and prompt fatalities in the public depends on the meteorological conditions during and immediately following the release and the energy content of the release.

A large radioactive release during favorable meteorological conditions may not have the potential for causing prompt fatalities in the public. The opposite is possible if releases occurred during unfavorable meteorological conditions. In a PRA framework, many alternative meteorological conditions are used (based on actual site data), some of which are favorable and some of which are unfavorable so that the effect of virtually all meteorological scenarios can be represented.

A release accompanied by a large quantity of thermal energy may result in the plume lifting off from the building wake and rising in the atmosphere while being transported by the wind, resulting in low offsite doses. This happened during the release from the Chernobyl accident and, therefore, there were no offsite prompt fatalities.

Comment: After the Chernobyl accident, it is difficult to justify a lack of accounting of doses beyond 50 miles in the risk calculations.

Response:

In draft NUREG–1150, the radiological consequence calculations were limited to 500 miles from a damaged reactor. In the analysis for the present version of the report, all radioactive material (except for the noble gases) remaining in the plume at 500 miles from the plant was deposited on the ground between 500 miles and 1,000 miles from the reactor. The contribution of all pathways of exposure between 500 and 1,000 miles are also included in the estimates of the consequences. This ensures nearly 100 percent accounting of the released radionuclides in the consequence calculations. The impact of the small quantities of noble gases leaving the 1,000-mile region is negligible.

Comment: It should be made clear that variations in the relocation/decontamination/interdiction dose criteria are included in the cost uncertainties.

Response:

Uncertainties in the offsite consequence models and the values of the input parameters to the consequence code were not treated in the previous analyses. In those analyses, the long-term relocation criterion of the Reactor Safety Study (Ref. D.7) of 25 rems in 30 years from groundshine was used. In the current analyses, the relocation criterion of 4 rems in 5 years from groundshine is used for base case calculations; this criterion is an approximation of the criterion currently proposed by the U. S. Environmental Protection Agency (Ref. D.59). The criterion found in the Reactor Safety Study is also used in the current calculations but only to show the sensitivity of the long-term health effects.

Comment: More discussion is needed on the assumptions that have been made about relocation and time scales for the decontamination of property after the 7-day emergency phase when doses could still be high.

Response:

In the current consequence calculations, decontamination of both land and buildings was assumed to reduce the levels of radioactive material by a factor of three or 15. A reduction by a factor of three was assumed to require 60 days of decontamination work; a reduction by a factor of 15 was assumed to require 120 days of decontamination work. The decontamination efforts were assumed to commence at the end of the 7-day emergency phase. The affected people were assumed to be relocated during the decontamination period.

D.8 Uses of NUREG–1150 As a Resource Document

D.8.1 Uses

Comment: The way that NUREG–1150 will be factored into the regulatory process is unclear.

Response:

NUREG–1150 is not intended to represent a quantitative and systematic evaluation of regulations. However, NUREG–1150 does provide a source of information that can support, at least in part, such an objective. The document provides an information base for analyzing plant-specific and generic safety issues. The NUREG–1150 models can be used for assessing the safety significance of operational occurrences and as a basis for evaluating alternative design changes to improve safety. A discussion of the use of NUREG–1150 in the regulatory process is provided in Chapter 13 of NUREG–1150 and in Reference D.8.

Comment: Risk assessment offers a logical framework to review regulations and examine safety issues. The decision to use risk assessment as a basis for regulatory decisionmaking is a major advancement in the regulation of nuclear power plants. But regulators need to be fully aware of the strengths and the weaknesses of their tools and to be concerned with the degree of precision needed to ensure safety.

Response:

NUREG–1150 is not intended to represent a quantitative and systematic evaluation of regulations. However, NUREG–1150 does provide an information source that can support such an objective. The results in NUREG–1150 will be used with full recognition of the uncertainties involved and the strengths and the weaknesses of the methods from which the results were derived (as described in Chapters 1 and 13).

Comment: The interpretation of expert judgments about containment response in terms of probabilities has a large effect on risk estimates. The NUREG–1150 study suggests that the major contributor to risk is early containment failure, but the large uncertainty precludes any regulatory decision on the need for risk reduction using, for example, venting strategies, refractory-lined cavities, and in-plant emergency procedures.

Response:

There are necessarily large uncertainties associated with severe accident risks. These large uncertainties are due in part to a lack of understanding associated with many of the complex phenomena in severe accidents. The uncertainty in risk does not preclude its use in decisionmaking. Decisions must be made in spite of the uncertainties, but the uncertainties may change the type of decision being made.

Comment: The application of NUREG–1150 should be discontinued until the risk estimates are improved.

Response:

Draft NUREG–1150 has not been widely used as a basis for regulatory action during the comment period or while modifications were under way. However, the interim findings of the draft report and the methods developed were not completely ignored. Rather, items identified as being potentially important in the draft report were considered in developing the listing of items for consideration in the guidance provided for the individual plant examination process. Similarly, the information on containment performance provided one input into the NRC's containment performance improvement study. The draft NUREG–1150 information provided a starting point for the development of a more focused in-depth analysis of various issues. As discussed in Chapter 13, the future uses envisaged for NUREG–1150 do not rely heavily on the quantitative results obtained for the five plants analyzed.

D.8.2 Cost/Benefit Analysis

Comment: The models used in calculating the cost of a severe accident lack many factors that should be taken into account. Many of the assumptions are questionable and unfounded. The models have not been benchmarked. Some interpretations and conclusions that were made in draft NUREG–1150 are questionable. The cost estimates need to be more thoroughly documented to understand and evaluate the calculations.

Response:

The present version of NUREG–1150 provides a limited set of risk-reduction calculations, principally related to the potential benefits of accident management strategies in reducing core damage frequency. It does not assess the costs of these or other improvements. Such analyses are more properly considered in the context of specific regulatory actions.

Comment: The averted cost (in terms of risk reduction) does not include secondary costs. The draft risk study recognizes that secondary costs may significantly increase the benefit of some safety options but no attempt was made to quantify this increase. The underestimate can be attributed to the following:

1. The cost of shutdowns of similar reactors on the same site and at other sites.

2. The possibility of a moratorium on nuclear power due to a severe accident.

3. The value of $1 million per averted acute fatality and $100,000 per latent cancer fatality may be too low.

4. The values of the interdiction dose used in the calculations may be too high.

5. No allowance has been made for the decrease in long-term value of land and buildings that have been contaminated.

6. Decontamination costs used in the calculations may be based on decontamination of test sites in deserts instead of agricultural, residential, and commercial property.

7. The radiation releases are calculated out to 50 miles; a radius as much as 500 miles may be more appropriate.

Response:

The draft NUREG–1150 cost/benefit analyses reflected the conventional NRC methods for assessing costs and benefits. Because cost/benefit analyses are more properly considered in the context of specific regulatory activities, they are not provided in this version of NUREG–1150.

D.8.3 Safety Goal Comparisons

Comment: NUREG–1150 finds that the U.S. safety goals are met; this discourages further improvements in safety.

Response:

As discussed in Chapter 13, this version of NUREG–1150 indicates that the five plants studied in NUREG–1150 are below the Commission's quantitative health objectives. The NRC staff disagrees that the findings of NUREG–1150 discourage further improvements in nuclear safety. Many improvements have been made at the five plants studied in NUREG–1150 since the draft report was first published in February 1987; some of the safety improvements arose from this study of various features of the five plants. The NRC staff believes that a comprehensive risk analysis on a plant enhances safety because it presents an overall and comprehensive view of interactions among plant systems and operator actions. Similarly, the variety of perspectives drawn in NUREG–1150, particularly in Chapters 8 and 12, provide information that other plants may consider as they perform individual plant examinations.

D.8.4 Extrapolation of Results

Comment: It is unclear how NUREG–1150 will be used in conjunction with individual plant evaluations or plant-specific PRAs as a basis for regulatory decisionmaking.

Response:

Perspectives gained from NUREG–1150, previous industry-sponsored PRAs, and analyses done by industry groups, such as IDCOR's analysis of four containment configurations, have been assembled into several NRC reports (Ref. D.60). These reports provide information to the analysts performing individual plant examinations (IPEs) concerning plant features and operator actions that are important to the evaluation of risk. Chapter 13 discusses how NUREG–1150 is used in the IPE; details of the IPE process are presented in Reference D.61.

REFERENCES FOR APPENDIX D

D.1 U. S. Nuclear Regulatory Commission (USNRC), "Draft NUREG–1150 for Public Comment: Issuance and Availability," *Federal Register*, Vol. 52, p. 7950, March 13, 1987.

D.2 USNRC, "Seminar on Methodology Used in NUREG–1150, 'Reactor Risk Reference Document'," *Federal Register*, Vol. 52, p. 8390, March 17, 1987.

D.3 ACRS, "ACRS Comments on Draft NUREG–1150, 'Reactor Risk Reference Document'," letter from W. Kerr, Chairman, Advisory Committee on Reactor Safeguards, to L. W. Zech, Chairman, USNRC, July 1987. ACRS, "Report on NUREG–1150, 'Reactor Risk Reference Document'," letter from W. Kerr, Chairman, Advisory Committee on Reactor Safeguards, to L. W. Zech, Chairman, USNRC, August 16, 1988. ACRS, "NUREG–1150: Resolution of ACRS Comments," letter from F. Remick, Chairman, Advisory Committee on Reactor Safeguards, to L. W. Zech, Chairman, USNRC, January 23, 1989.

D.4 H. J. C. Kouts et al., "Methodology for Uncertainty Estimation in NUREG–1150 (Draft): Conclusions of a Review Panel," Brookhaven National Laboratory, NUREG/CR–5000, BNL–NUREG–52119, December 1987.

D.5 W. E. Kastenberg et al., "Findings of the Peer Review Panel on the Draft Reactor Risk Reference Document, NUREG–1150," Lawrence Livermore National Laboratory, NUREG/CR–5113, UCID–21346, May 1988.

D.6 L. LeSage et al., "Initial Report of the Special Committee on Reactor Risk Reference Document (NUREG–1150)," American Nuclear Society, April 1988.

D.7 USNRC, "Reactor Safety Study—An Assessment of Accident Risks in U.S. Commercial Nuclear Power Plants," WASH–1400 (NUREG–75/014), October 1975.

D.8 USNRC, "Integration Plan for Closure of Severe Accident Issues," SECY–88–147, May 25, 1988.

D.9 J. S. Evans et al., "On the Propagation of Error in Air Pollution Measurements," *Environmental Monitoring and Assessment*, Vol. 4, pp. 139–53, 1984.

D.10 H. W. Lewis et al., "Risk Assessment Review Group Report to the U.S. Nuclear Regulatory Commission," Ad Hoc Review Group, NUREG/CR–0400, September 1978.

D.11 D. I. Chanin , H. Jow, J. A. Rollstin et al., "MELCOR Accident Consequence Code System (MACCS)," Sandia National Laboratories, NUREG/CR–4691, Vols. 1–3, SAND86–1562, February 1990.

D.12 R. J. Breeding et al., "Evaluation of Severe Accident Risks: Surry Unit 1," Sandia National Laboratories, NUREG/CR–4551, Vol. 3, Revision 1, SAND86–1309, October 1990.

D.13 A. C. Payne, Jr., et al., "Evaluation of Severe Accident Risks: Peach Bottom Unit 2," Sandia National Laboratories, NUREG/CR–4551, Vol. 4, Revision 1, SAND86–1309, December 1990.

D.14 J. J. Gregory et al., "Evaluation of Severe Accident Risks: Sequoyah Unit 1," Sandia National Laboratories, NUREG/CR–4551, Vol. 5, Revision 1, SAND86–1309, December 1990.

D.15 T. D. Brown et al., "Evaluation of Severe Accident Risks: Grand Gulf Unit 1," Sandia National Laboratories, NUREG/CR–4551, Vol. 6, Revision 1, SAND86–1309, December 1990

D.16 C. K. Park et al., "Evaluation of Severe Accident Risks: Zion Unit 1," Brookhaven National Laboratory, NUREG/CR–4551, Vol. 7, Draft Revision 1, BNL–NUREG–52029, to be published.*

D.17 D. B. Clauss, "Round-Robin Analysis of the Behavior of a 1:6-Scale Reinforced Concrete Containment Model Pressurized to Failure: Posttest Evaluations," Sandia National Laboratories, NUREG/CR–5341, SAND89–0349, October 1989.

*Available in the NRC Public Document Room, 2120 L Street NW., Washington, DC.

D.18 F. T. Harper et al., "Evaluation of Severe Accident Risks: Quantification of Major Input Parameters," Sandia National Laboratories, NUREG/CR–4551, Vol. 2, Revision 1, SAND86–1309, December 1990.

D.19 R. C. Bertucio and J. A. Julius, "Analysis of Core Damage Frequency: Surry Unit 1," Sandia National Laboratories, NUREG/CR–4550, Vol. 3, Revision 1, SAND86–2084, April 1990.

D.20 A. M. Kolaczkowski et al., "Analysis of Core Damage Frequency: Peach Bottom Unit 2," Sandia National Laboratories, NUREG/CR–4550, Vol. 4, Revision 1, SAND86–2084, August 1989.

D.21 R. C. Bertucio and S. R. Brown, "Analysis of Core Damage Frequency: Sequoyah Unit 1," Sandia National Laboratories, NUREG/CR–4550, Vol. 5, Revision 1, SAND86–2084, April 1990.

D.22 M. T. Drouin et al., "Analysis of Core Damage Frequency: Grand Gulf Unit 1," Sandia National Laboratories, NUREG/CR–4550, Vol. 6, Revision 1, SAND86–2084, September 1989.

D.23 M. B. Sattison and K. W. Hall, "Analysis of Core Damage Frequency: Zion Unit 1," Idaho National Engineering Laboratory, NUREG/CR–4550, Vol. 7, Revision 1, EGG–2554, May 1990.

D.24 M. Silberberg et al., "Reassessment of the Technical Bases for Estimating Source Terms," USNRC Report NUREG–0956, July 1986.

D.25 K. D. Bergeron et al., "User's Manual for CONTAIN 1.0, A Computer Code for Severe Reactor Accident Containment Analysis," Sandia National Laboratories, NUREG/CR–4085, SAND84–1204, July 1985.

D.26 R. M. Summers et al., "MELCOR In-Vessel Modeling," *Proceedings of the Fifteenth Water Reactor Safety Information Meeting* (Gaithersburg, MD), NUREG/CP–0091, February 1988.

D.27 S. S. Dosanjh (Ed.), "MELPROG-PWR/MOD1: A Two-Dimensional, Mechanistic Code for Analysis of Reactor Core Melt Progression and Vessel Attack Under Severe Accident Conditions," Sandia National Laboratories, NUREG/CR–5193, SAND88–1824, May 1989.

D.28 R. L. Iman and M. J. Shortencarier, "A Fortran 77 Program and User's Guide for the Generation of Latin Hypercube and Random Samples for Use with Computer Models," Sandia National Laboratories, NUREG/CR–3624, SAND83–2365, June 1984.

D.29 M. L. Corradini et al., "A Review of the Severe Accident Risk Reduction Program (SARRP) Containment Event Trees," University of Wisconsin, NUREG/CR–4569, May 1986.

D.30 P. Cybulskis, "Assessment of the XSOR Codes," Battelle Columbus Division, NUREG/CR–5346, BMI–2171, November 1989.

D.31 R. L. Iman et al., "PARTITION: A Program for Defining the Source Term/Consequence Analysis Interfaces in the NUREG–1150 Probabilistic Risk Assessments," Sandia National Laboratories, NUREG/CR–5253, SAND88–2940, May 1990.

D.32 E. D. Gorham-Bergeron et al., "Evaluation of Severe Accident Risks: Methodology for the Accident Progression, Source Term, Consequence, Risk Integration, and Uncertainty Analyses," Sandia National Laboratories, NUREG/CR–4551, Vol. 1, Draft Revision 1, SAND86–1309, to be published.*

D.33 U. Tveten, "Review of the Chronic Exposure Pathway Models in MACCS and Several Other Well-Known Probabilistic Risk Assessment Models," Institutt for Energiteknikk, Norway, NUREG/CR–5377, June 1990.

D.34 Commonwealth Edison Company of Chicago, "Zion Probabilistic Safety Study," September 1981.

D.35 USNRC, "Nuclear Power Plant Severe Accident Research Plan" (G. P. Marino, Ed.), NUREG–0900, Revision 1, April 1986.

D.36 R. Wilson et al., "Report to the APS of the Study Group on Radionuclide Release from Severe Accidents at Nuclear Power Plants," *Reviews of Modern Physics*, Vol. 57, No. 3, Part II, July 1985.

*Available in the NRC Public Document Room, 2120 L Street NW., Washington, DC.

D.37 D. L. Berry et al., "Review and Evaluation of the Zion Probabilistic Safety Study: Plant Analysis," Sandia National Laboratories, NUREG/CR–3300, Vol. 1, SAND83–1118, May 1984.

D.38 D. M. Ericson, Jr., (Ed.) et al., "Analysis of Core Damage Frequency: Internal Events Methodology," Sandia National Laboratories, NUREG/CR–4550, Vol. 1, Revision 1, SAND86–2084, January 1990.

D.39 T. A. Wheeler et al., "Analysis of Core Damage Frequency from Internal Events: Expert Judgment Elicitation," Sandia National Laboratories, NUREG/CR–4550, Vol. 2, SAND86–2084, April 1989.

D.40 R. M. Harrington and L. C. Fuller, "BWR-LTAS: A Boiling Water Reactor Long-Term Accident Simulation Code," Oak Ridge National Laboratory, NUREG/CR–3764, ORNL/TM–9163, February 1985.

D.41 W. J. Luckas, Jr., "A Human Reliability Analysis for the ATWS Accident Sequence with MSIV Closure at the Peach Bottom Atomic Power Station," Brookhaven National Laboratory, May 1986.

D.42 Fauske and Associates, Inc., "MAAP Modular Accident Analysis Program User's Manual," Vols. I and II, IDCOR Technical Report 16.2–3, February 1987.

D.43 D. J. Hanson et al., "Containment Venting Analysis for the Peach Bottom Atomic Power Station," Battelle Columbus Laboratories, NUREG/CR–4696, EGG–2464, February 1987.

D.44 USNRC, "A Review of the Current Understanding for the Potential for Containment Failure from In-Vessel Steam Explosions," NUREG–1116, June 1985.

D.45 D. A. Powers et al., "VANESA: A Mechanistic Model of Radionuclide Release and Aerosol Generation During Core Debris Interactions with Concrete," Sandia National Laboratories, NUREG/CR–4308, SAND85–1370, July 1986.

D.46 F. Muir et al., "CORCON-MOD1: An Improved Model for Core/Concrete Interactions," Sandia National Laboratories, NUREG/CR–2142, SAND80–2415, September 1981.

D.47 R. K. Cole, Jr., et al., "CORCON-MOD2: A Computer Program for Analysis of Molten-Core Concrete Interactions," Sandia National Laboratories, NUREG/CR–3920, SAND84–1246, October 1984.

D.48 E. C. Beahm et al., "Calculations of Iodine Source Terms in Support of NUREG–0956," Oak Ridge National Laboratory, ORNL/NRC/LTR–86/17, Technical Letter Report, July 1986.

D.49 G. A. Berna et al., "RELAP5/SCDAP/MOD0 Code Manual," EGG–RTH–7051, EG&G, September 1985.

D.50 T. S. Kress, "Review of the Status of Validation of the Computer Codes Used in the Severe Accident Source Term Reassessment Study (BMI–2104)," Oak Ridge National Laboratory, ORNL/TM–8842, April 1985.

D.51 M. Khatib-Rahbar et al., "Independent Verification of Radionuclide Release Calculations for Selected Accident Scenarios," Brookhaven National Laboratory, NUREG/CR–4629, BNL–NUREG–51998, July 1986.

D.52 R. O. Wooton, "MARCH Calculations Performed for the TMI-2 Analysis Exercise," *Nuclear Technology*, Vol. 87, August 1989.

D.53 D. W. Akers et al., "TMI-2 Core Debris Grab Samples—Examination and Analysis, Part 1," Idaho National Engineering Laboratory, GEND-INF–075, p. 110, September 1986.

D.54 S. Acharya et al., "Benchmarking of the MACCS Code," *Transactions of the American Nuclear Society* (San Diego, California), Vol. 56, pp. 353–4, June 12–16, 1988.

D.55 S. Acharya et al., "Benchmarking of the MACCS Code," *Proceedings of the Second Part of the Joint CEC/OECD/NEA Workshop on Recent Advances in Reactor Accident Consequent Assessment* (Rome, Italy), pp. 50–2, January 25–29, 1988.

D.56 C. A. Dobbe et al., "Quality Assurance and Verification of the MACCS Code, Version 1.5," Idaho National Engineering Laboratory, NUREG/CR-5376, EGG-2566, February 1990.

D.57 The Federal Minister of Research and Technology, "The German Risk Study—Summary," Gesellschaft fur Reaktorsicherheit (Germany), August 15, 1979.

D.58 M. R. Hayes et al., "The Technical Basis of 'Spectral Source Terms' for Assessing Uncertainties in Fission Product Release During Accidents in PWRs with Special Reference to Sizewell-B," United Kingdom Atomic Energy Authority, SRD-R-256, November 1982.

D.59 U.S. Environmental Protection Agency, "Manual of Protective Action Guides and Protective Actions for Nuclear Incidents," Office of Radiation Programs, Draft, 1989.

D.60 Brookhaven National Laboratory, "Assessment of Severe Accident Prevention and Mitgation Features," NUREG/CR-4920, Vols. 1-5, BNL-NUREG-52070, July 1988.

D.61 NRC Letter to All Licensees Holding Operating Licenses and Construction Permits for Nuclear Power Reactor Facilities, "Individual Plant Examination for Severe Accident Vulnerabilities—10 CFR §50.54f," Generic Letter 88-20, dated November 23, 1988.

APPENDIX E

RESPONSE TO COMMENTS
ON SECOND DRAFT OF NUREG-1150

CONTENTS

TABLES

E.1 Introduction

In June 1989, the NRC published NUREG–1150, "Severe Accident Risks: An Assessment for Five U.S. Nuclear Power Plants," as a second draft for peer review (Ref. E.1). At that time, the NRC also formed a peer review committee under the provisions of the Federal Advisory Committee Act to review the second draft report and answer certain questions with respect to its adequacy. This committee was chaired by Dr. Herbert J.C. Kouts; its entire membership is shown in Table E.1. In parallel, the American Nuclear Society (ANS) continued its review of the report, using a special committee of ANS members. This committee was chaired by Dr. Leo G. LeSage; its entire membership is shown in Table E.2. The comments of both committees were provided to the staff in the summer of 1990 (Refs. E.2 and E.3). This appendix summarizes the comments of the NRC-established committee (the "Kouts Committee") and the ANS committee. Summary staff responses are provided for each specific comment.

The second draft of NUREG–1150 has also been the subject of review by the NRC's Advisory Committee on Reactor Safeguards (ACRS). Its technical review was completed in October 1990; a letter providing its comments was submitted on November 15, 1990. This letter is provided as an attachment to this appendix.

Public comment was also requested on the second draft of NUREG–1150. Four comment letters were received (Refs. E.4 through E.7). These comments have also been assessed and, where appropriate, changes made in the final version of NUREG–1150.

Before discussing the comments provided by the committees on particular topics, it is worth describing the overall conclusions and findings expressed in their reports.

The overall conclusions of the Kouts committee were:

- "NUREG–1150 is a good report, and it represents a great deal of detailed high-quality work. It is commendable that an endeavor was made to consult a wider range of competence apart from that possessed by those directly engaged in producing NUREG–1150. The benefit of constructive openness to criticism is felt in the revised draft."

- "NUREG–1150 draws upon a decade and a half of practice of PSA [probabilistic safety analysis] beyond WASH–1400, mainly in the United States but also in other countries. In most respects, it represents the state of the art of this kind of analysis. It is a step forward from WASH–1400."

- "The data drawn on include many years of experience in plant operation, and a similar period of theoretical and experimental research into severe accident methodology."

- "The disciplined use of expert opinion elicitation was an important advance over previous methods of using expert opinion. It is noted that the prime motive of this technique was to assess the uncertainty in the results of the PSA."

- "The results were derived in great detail, and they are presented by methods which show well their probabilistic spread."

- "NUREG–1150 should be a valuable source of data and methodology to guide future PSAs for individual plants. Like its predecessor, WASH–1400, it should help to show the path for future PSA developments for some time to come." (Kouts 7.2)

The overall findings of the ANS committee review were:

- "NUREG–1150 is a major achievement."

- "The revised draft reports essentially a new study."

- "The revised draft provides a balanced presentation of the central tendencies and uncertainties in risk."

Table E.1 'Membership of Special Committee to Review the Severe Accident Risks Report.

Herbert J.C. Kouts	Committee Chairman, Defense Nuclear Facility Safety Board
George Apostolakis	University of California, Los Angeles
E.H. Adolf Birkhofer	Gesellschaft fur Reaktorsicherheit Forschungsgelande, Federal Republic of Germany
Lars G. Hoegberg	Swedish Nuclear Power Inspectorate
William G. Kastenberg	University of California, Los Angeles
Leo G. LeSage	Argonne National Laboratory
Norman C. Rasmussen	Massachusetts Institute of Technology
Harry J. Teague	Safety and Reliability Directorate, United Kingdom Atomic Energy Authority
John J. Taylor	Electric Power Research Institute

Table E.2 Membership of American Nuclear Society Special Committee on NUREG-1150.

Leo G. LeSage	Committee Chairman, Argonne National Laboratory
Edward A. Warman	Committee Vice Chairman, Stone & Webster Engineering Corporation
Richard C. Anoba	Carolina Power and Light Company*
Ronald K. Bayer	Virginia Power Company**
R. Allan Brown	Ontario Hydro, Canada
James C. Carter, III	Tenera Risk Management
J. Peter Hosemann	Paul Scherrer Institute, Switzerland
W. Reed Johnson	University of Virginia
Walter B. Loewenstein	Electric Power Research Institute***
Nicholas Tsoulfanidis	University of Missouri
Willem F. Vinck	Associated Consultant, Belgium****

---

* Currently with Science Applications International Corporation.
** Member in 1987 and 1988.
*** Member until June 1989.
**** Corresponding member.

- "The use of expert opinion in the revised study was greatly improved."

- "NUREG-1150 should supplant WASH-1400."

- "The NRC safety goals are shown to be met for all five plants studied."

- "The NUREG-1150 documentation is a useful compendium of current severe accident analysis information and data."

- "The quality of the report is substantially improved."

- "[The report] is adequate for its stated uses."

The general comments of the ACRS were:

- "We have reviewed the reports prepared by the ANS Special Committee and by the Special Committee to Review the Severe Accident Risk Report appointed by the Commission [the Kouts Committee] and found them helpful. We have no serious disagreements with either of these reviews, nor with their findings."

- "The work described in this [second] draft of NUREG–1150 is an improvement over that described in the first version entitled, 'Reactor Risk Reference Document.' Many previously identified deficiencies in the expert elicitation process have been corrected. The exposition and organization of the report have been improved. The presentation of results is clearer. There is considerable information that was not in the original version."

- "The portion that deals with accident initiation and development up to the point at which core heat removal can no longer be assured is unique, compared to other contemporary PRAs, in that a method for estimating the uncertainty in the results has been developed and applied. This method and its application are significant contributions. Although the larger contributions to uncertainty in risk come from the later parts of the accident sequences, this portion is enhanced also by an extensive identification of events that can serve as accident initiators as well as an associated set of hypothesized event trees. This information should be of considerable assistance to licensees in the performance of an Individual Plant Examination (IPE). It should also be useful to plant operators and to designers."

- "The formulation of a more detailed representation of accident progression after severe core damage begins, and an improved description of containment performance, contribute some additional information to this important area. However, understanding of many of the physical phenomena that have an important bearing on this phase of accident progression is still very sparse, and the report may give the impression that more is known about this portion of the accident sequence than is actually the case."

- "The part of the sequence that begins with the release of radioactive material outside the containment is treated by a relatively new and unevaluated code system. Furthermore, there is no estimate of the uncertainties inherent in the calculations that describe this part of the sequence. Those who use the quantitative values of reported risk must recognize that these uncertainties are not accounted for in the calculated results."

The ACRS letter contained two other comments of particular note. These were:

- "It is disappointing that the staff asserts that virtually no general conclusions can be drawn from a study that took almost five years and seventeen million dollars to complete. We recommend that the Commission encourage the staff to mine more deeply the wealth of information that has been collected in the course of this study in an effort to identify generic conclusions that might be reached."

- The NUREG–1150 "results should be used only by those who have a thorough understanding of its limitations."

These last comments are discussed in Section E.8 ("Uses of NUREG–1150"). Specific limitations noted in the ACRS letter are discussed throughout this appendix.

The remaining sections of this appendix provide itemizations of comments (including more specific findings of the ANS committee) received from the review committees and the ACRS on the second draft of NUREG–1150 and staff responses. Comments relating to two general areas, scope and documentation, are itemized first (in Sections E.2 and E.3), followed by comments on specific technical areas: use of expert judgment; accident frequency analysis; accident progression analysis; and source term and offsite consequence analysis (in Sections E.4 through E.7). Finally, Section E.8 itemizes comments on the uses of NUREG–1150.

It should be noted that all committees concluded that issuance of the final version of NUREG–1150 should not be delayed for the conduct of further research or analysis. As such, the responses to certain comments indicate that issues requiring significant effort may be the subject of future NRC work rather than included in the final version of NUREG–1150.

E.2 Scope

Chapter 1 of the second draft of NUREG–1150 described the scope of the risk analyses and identified certain limitations of these analyses. The review committees also noted these limitations, as well as others. Some more general comments by the committees with respect to scope included:

- "The second draft of NUREG–1150 addressed many of the shortcomings identified in the first draft and it provided a more comprehensive and incisive view of risk from the existing light water reactors than did WASH–1400." (Kouts 4.1)

- "In general, NUREG–1150 represents state-of-the-art methodology in PSA and associated uncertainty analysis. However, comparison of resulting risk figures between individual plants and with quantitative safety goals must be made with caution, taking into account questions as to the completeness of the analysis and uncertainties in methods and data." (Kouts 4.12) (Such reservations are itemized in the comments below.)

- "Many of the limitations and uncertainties mentioned above [in Section 4.12 of the Kouts report] may be reduced by improved PSA methodology and by improved experimental and empirical data. Such improvements should be made part of the IPE [Individual Plant Examination] program, but not delay it. We note that many such improvements in methods and data have become available since the closure date for the NUREG–1150 analysis." (Kouts 4.12)

The review committees also provided a number of more specific comments. These are itemized below and staff responses provided.

Comment: The list of initiating events was extensive, and, in most respects, state of the art, but it was not complete. Initiating events not considered included:

- Human errors of commission;

- Incidents starting from low power and shutdown conditions;

- Leaks or breaks of PWR steamlines; and

- Sabotage (understandable in view of methodological and other difficulties involved) (Kouts 3.2.1.1; ACRS).

The effects of aging were not included in the analysis (Kouts 4.12, 7.2).

Response:

The staff acknowledges that human errors of commission have not been included. The treatment of such errors has been the subject of considerable research for several years, but had not sufficiently evolved to permit its use when the NUREG–1150 risk analyses were initiated in 1985. The NRC is currently studying ways in which errors of commission can be practically included in future PRAs (Ref. E.8).

The staff acknowledges that accidents initiated during low power and shutdown operations have not been included in the NUREG–1150 analyses. Recent PRA studies and events in the United States and Europe indicate that the core damage frequency from accidents initiated in such plant operational modes may be significant. The NRC has initiated studies of low power and shutdown accident frequencies and risks for two of the NUREG–1150 plants, Surry and Grand Gulf. Interim, scoping results of these studies are expected in mid-1991. In addition, the NRC has initiated a more general review of non-full-power operational modes to identify the need for additional regulatory requirements. This review is scheduled to be completed in 1991.

Sabotage risks have not been included in the NUREG–1150 risk studies. While the effects of sabotage actions may be similar to that of accidents included in the risk studies, the estimation of the frequencies of such actions is highly uncertain and requires a detailed analysis of the spectrum of threats. Because this threat may be highly variable with time, the staff does not consider it meaningful to attempt to include sabotage risks in PRAs.

The potential for PWR steamline breaks to lead to core damage was assessed (using conservative screening analyses) and determined to be of little significance in the NUREG–1150 PWRs. For some break locations, a steamline break can be similar to a loss of power conversion system transient event and thus can be subsumed into that event. For other break locations, steamline breaks can be recovered through any one of several methods (e.g., feed and bleed cooling, or use of crossties of auxiliary feedwater or emergency core cooling injection from a second unit, if such crossties exist). Using such logic, the core damage potential resulting from such events was judged to be of sufficiently low frequency that it could be screened out early in the analysis. It should be noted, however, that steamline breaks could be important in other PWRs with different plant layouts and system redundancy.

Aging effects were not explicitly included in the analyses. Some consideration of such effects occurs indirectly, however, in that the data base of component and other failures includes failures resulting from aging. The NRC has an extensive program to investigate the impact of aging on plant equipment and to develop and test methods for more explicitly including aging effects in PRA. This work is described in Reference E.9.

Chapter 1 of NUREG-1150 has been updated to better reflect these comments on limitations of the risk analyses.

Comment: The Kouts committee had reservations with respect to the completeness of modeling of inter-dependencies of technical systems, including detailed modeling of auxiliary systems, formally regarded as not safety-related (Kouts 4.12).

Response:

A major portion of the analysis was devoted to accurately modeling the important auxiliary/support systems, such as component cooling water, and normal and emergency service water. Dependency matrices were developed to identify the dependence of each frontline system on such systems. Connections between safety and nonsafety systems, such as connections to electric power buses, were explicitly considered. Failures of the support systems were also explicitly considered as initiating events. Although most of these events could be ruled out (in initial screening analyses) as initiating events because of train separation, the use of alternative systems, and operator recovery actions, failures of some support systems did contribute to the estimated core damage frequencies (e.g., the component cooling water system failure at Zion and some electric power bus failures).

Comment: The Kouts committee had reservations with respect to uncertainties associated with probabilities mainly based on expert judgment, especially where considerable divergence of opinion existed (Kouts 4.12).

Response:

This comment is discussed in Section E.4.

Comment: The Kouts committee had reservations with respect to the impact of "safety culture" and the fact that the potential effects of management quality are not included (Kouts 4.12).

Response:

This comment is discussed in Section E.5.1.

Comment: Users of the report should be aware of assumptions made in the screening process in which low frequency accident sequences were eliminated from further consideration and that it may not be appropriate to screen out potential sequences in other plants based on the NUREG-1150 studies (ACRS).

Response:

The staff agrees with this comment.

Comment: The frequency of disruptive failure of the reactor pressure vessel was estimated to be between 1E-7 and 1E-6 per reactor year, yet the event was not treated in the analysis. Reviews published in recent years indicate failure probabilities typically in the range of 1E-6 to 1E-9 per reactor year based mainly on probabilistic fracture mechanics considerations. These considerations show a significant influence of plant-specific parameters such as material properties and aging, positioning of welds, and inspection programs. Thus, a somewhat more extensive discussion might have been warranted in NUREG-1150 (Kouts 3.2.1.7).

Response:

A limited screening analysis was performed for NUREG–1150 which indicated that the relative contribution of vessel rupture to core damage frequency would be negligible. For this reason, this issue was not pursued further.

One issue that could have a significant effect on the estimated core damage frequencies of PWRs due to pressure vessel rupture is pressurized thermal shock (PTS). In 1985, the NRC issued new regulations (Ref. E.10), and defined a screening criterion, to limit the potential impact of PTS. Estimates have been made as to when each licensed PWR would reach this screening criterion (Ref. E.11); none of the three PWRs studied in NUREG–1150 is close to reaching this criterion.

Comment: The lack of analysis of external events for three of the plants studied is a deficiency (Kouts 7.2).

The fire analysis in NUREG–1150 was limited to Surry and Peach Bottom. It was generally state of the art but should have been extended to all five plants (Kouts 4.3.3, 7.2).

Response:

The original intent of (what was to become) the NUREG–1150 risk analyses was to provide perspectives on the mid-1980's revisions to source term technology and thus early analyses did not include accidents initiated by external events. In response to comments on the first draft report, the risk analyses of two plants were extended to include external-event analyses. All five plants were not subjected to external-event analyses because of time and budget constraints. The staff concurs, however, with the basic point made that modern PRAs should include consideration of externally initiated accidents.

Comment: Although the two seismic PRAs in NUREG–1150 have been carried through Level 3, these results have not been reported. We believe that these results might provide valuable insights about seismic vulnerabilities of containment systems (ACRS).

Response:

As discussed in Chapter 1, the seismic risk calculations are not described in NUREG–1150 because of certain issues relating to the nonradiological consequences of large earthquakes. While some data are provided in NUREG–1150 with respect to containment performance during seismic events, detailed information is provided in supporting contractor reports (Refs. E.12 and E.13).

Comment: The methods and data used [in the fire analysis] were probably the best available at the time the work was performed. However, certain issues identified more recently may result in increased fire risk estimates (ACRS).

Response:

The staff agrees that the more recently identified issues could be significant. The staff is currently investigating these issues further with respect to their importance to plant safety. As the results of these investigations become clear, the staff will reassess the adequacy of current PRA methods and, if appropriate, initiate work to improve the methods.

Comment: It is not clear as to why loss of instrument air was judged not to be important (Kouts 3.2.1.1).

Response:

The loss of instrument air was examined as a potential initiating event. The plants were examined to determine: if the loss of instrument air resulted in a plant trip and the need for decay heat removal; and the effects of loss of instrument air on accident prevention and mitigation systems. For the plants considered, this event was examined and determined to be of minimal importance. Reasons for this conclusion included plant-specific design features such as separation of air supplies, coupled with the availability of backup systems, and/or that loss of instrument air resulted in plant conditions similar to those of other initiating event groups of higher frequencies, such as a transient with the loss of the power conversion system.

Comment: Recognizing and supporting NRC's desire to publish a final NUREG-1150, we recommend that the report indicate the likely impact of Commonwealth Edison Company's committed modifications on the Zion plant results (Kouts 4.2.2).

Response:

The NRC staff has identified the specific modifications that have now been made to the Zion plant (Ref. E.14). Using this information, sensitivity studies have been performed to assess a revised mean core damage frequency and risk for the Zion plant. Chapters 7, 8, and 12 have been revised to indicate the impact of the modifications made at Zion. More detailed documentation of the sensitivity studies performed is provided in Section 15 of Appendix C.

E.3 Documentation and Display of Results

As discussed in Appendix D, the display of results in the first draft of NUREG-1150 was the subject of considerable controversy. Because of the displays used (and other reasons), the first draft was considered inscrutable. In response, the second draft of NUREG-1150 made significant changes to the displays. Some general comments made by the two review committees on this subject included:

- "[With respect to display of results,] the second draft, reviewed by this [Kouts] committee, followed a more conventional course, showing the probability distributions and the major parameters. This choice responds well to the criticisms of both WASH-1400 and the first draft of NUREG-1150, and the present Committee endorses the decision." (Kouts 4.11.1)

- "The current version does a much better job of presenting the results. A particularly helpful form of the results are the matrix-like figures in which mean values of accident progression bins are combined with mean plant damage states and their frequencies. Pie charts are used effectively to display qualitatively the contributions of various initiating events and accident progression scenarios." (ANS 2.a.12.c)

A related question to the choice of display techniques is the appropriateness of citing and using mean values (vs. median values) to describe uncertain parameters. The NRC-sponsored committee addressed this question and noted the following:

- "There has been much discussion over the matter of preference between use of the mean and the median as a point indicator in such cases. Which is the one that most accurately represents the full distribution? We leap forward to the answer: the preference depends on the precise question being asked. In some applications the mean would be preferred; in others it might be the median. There may be instances in which neither would suffice." (Kouts 4.11.3)

Some other general issues related to documentation were also addressed by the committees. These were:

- The (ANS) committee agrees with the decision not to include the radiological consequences of seismic events (ANS 2.a.9.b).

- The ANS committee agrees with the deletion of the analyses of accident prevention and mitigation features (ANS 2.a.10).

- The Kouts committee notes that the staff presentation of the Peach Bottom ATWS sequence demonstrated good traceability of the methods and data used in the analysis, as did the detailed documentation of the Grand Gulf case (Kouts 4.8.4).

The review committees also provided a number of more specific comments. These are itemized below and staff responses provided.

Comment: Experience shows that neglecting sequences with a frequency about two orders of magnitude below the calculated mean core damage frequency does not noticeably change the overall core damage frequency. Thus, for plants that have a mean core damage frequency of 1E-5 per year, a cutoff frequency of 1E-7 per year seems reasonable (Kouts 4.10.2).

It is reasonable to neglect individual risks that are about one order of magnitude or more below the value associated with the U.S. safety goals. A *de minimis* threshold of 1E-7 per year would appropriately represent this reasoning (Kouts 4.10.3).

Taking into account remaining uncertainties in the PRA methodology, e.g., with respect to completeness in the treatment of human factors and external events, estimated core damage frequencies much below 1E-5 per reactor year should be regarded with some caution (Kouts 4.12).

Response:

The staff basically agrees with the frequency cutoff suggested above. In general, accident sequences identified in NUREG-1150 as having frequencies roughly two orders of magnitude or lower below the accident sequence with the highest mean frequency were eliminated.

The staff also basically agrees with the suggestion of neglecting individual risks at levels one order of magnitude or more below the NRC safety goals. In some circumstances, however, values below such levels have been included in NUREG-1150 to permit comparisons with such risk measures as the frequency of a "large release" goal (see Section 13.2).

Chapter 1 has been modified to discuss the cautionary statements on interpretation of PRA results. Throughout the report, figures and tables have also been modified to indicate these cautions.

Comment: The last six chapters of the second draft of NUREG-1150 are the least effective and most difficult to follow portions of the report. Certain of the material is very worthwhile but much of the discussion seems forced, and the observations range from the obvious to those for which the analysis provides no apparent basis (ANS 2.a.12.d).

Response:

These chapters have been reviewed by the staff and its contractors and updated as appropriate. In addition, Appendix C has been expanded to provide additional discussion of issues important to the results and perspectives provided in Chapters 8 through 13.

Comment: Appendix B provides a valuable example of an accident sequence carried through from accident initiation to offsite consequence estimates. However, the example provided did not include early containment failure; hence many of the more interesting issues that are important to risk are not included in the discussion (ANS 5.e.2).

Response:

An example containing early containment failure was originally considered for Appendix B. The early containment failure example was considered interesting but, however, not typical. That is, a more typical sequence was chosen to avoid giving the wrong impression about the importance of early containment failure to risk at Surry. More detailed discussion of specific risk-important issues is provided separately in Appendix C.

Comment: The purpose of Appendix C was to provide some insight to the resolution of key issues. These discussions are sketchy and the information and reasoning that led to the expert judgments generally not provided. There seems to have been no concerted effort to provide a discussion of those issues that were most important to risk (ANS 5.e.1).

Response:

Appendix C has been reviewed and expanded to address other important issues. However, the information provided is still at a somewhat summary level. The reader seeking more detailed information than that in Appendix C should turn to the extensive issue discussions provided in References E.15 and E.16.

Comment: Recovery actions should be discussed in Chapter 2 and their impact quantified in Chapters 3 to 7 (Kouts 7.3).

Response:

Appendix A has been modified to clarify how recovery actions were treated in the risk studies. Important operator actions (including recovery actions) are addressed in qualitative terms in Chapters 3 through 7 along with other types of failures. The large number of events involved makes it impractical to provide discussion in the summary report. However, more detailed information, including sensitivity studies and importance calculations, is provided in Appendix C and in the plant-specific accident frequency analysis reports (Refs. E.17 through E.21).

Comment: To facilitate a comparison between estimates of offsite consequences in WASH-1400 and NUREG-1150, it is suggested that the final version of NUREG-1150 include comparisons of estimated probabilities of exceeding whole-body or thyroid doses as a function of distance from the site. These data are available from calculations already completed, so no delay in issuance of the report should be caused by incorporating such comparisons (Kouts 5.5; ANS 2.b.3, 2.b.10).

Response:

Although the consequence model used in NUREG-1150, MACCS 1.5 (Ref. E.22), can calculate center-line whole-body and thyroid doses as a function of distance from the site, neither of these specific results was generated and saved in the NUREG-1150 analyses. Thus, this information is not now available for generating dose versus distance plots. Because of the time required to develop such information and transform it into a form directly comparable with the Reactor Safety Study (Ref. E.23), it has not been included in the final version of NUREG-1150 but may be appropriate for study and publication in other forums.

Comment: The contributions of the unavailabilities of safety systems to the total core damage frequency should be displayed (Kouts 7.3).

Response:

The calculation and display of system unavailabilities is most appropriately performed on an accident sequence basis and should account for the operability states of support systems (e.g., the unavailability of the auxiliary feedwater system is different if ac power is or is not available). The staff believes that tabulating a single unavailability contribution (e.g., to core damage frequency) could thus be somewhat misleading and has chosen not to include such information in the final version of NUREG-1150. More detailed tabulations of system unavailabilities, accounting for support system availability, etc., could not be generated in a time period consistent with completion of the final report and thus have also not been included.

Comment: Since the supporting documentation upon which NUREG-1150 depends could be helpful to those performing an individual plant examination (IPE), these reports should be published as soon as feasible (ANS 2.b, ACRS).

Response:

Roughly 80 percent of the contractor reports supporting NUREG-1150 (including methods descriptions, computer code descriptions, and documentation of data and results) have now been published. The present staff and contractor schedules indicate publication of all reports by the end of March 1991.

Comment: In the plant-specific chapters, the substantial differences in the methods used for the Zion plant analysis are not highlighted (ANS 2.a.12.b).

Response:

Chapter 7 has been modified to highlight the differences in methods for the Zion accident frequency analysis.

Comment: The final version of NUREG-1150 should clearly state that it should be viewed as a new study and as a replacement for the first draft (ANS 2.b.6).

Response:

Chapter 1 has been modified to clearly state that the final version of NUREG–1150 is so different from the first draft that the latter should no longer be used.

Comment: The first draft of NUREG–1150 was better in one respect, in that it provided a schematic drawing of the containment and reactor coolant system in each plant-specific section (ANS 5.a).

Response:

Plant schematic diagrams have been added to each of the plant-specific chapters (i.e., Chapters 3 through 7).

Comment: Some presentations of results are so small, or so little contrast provided, that the results are unreadable (ANS 5.b).

Response:

Presentations of results throughout the report have been reviewed and improved where needed.

E.4 Use of Expert Judgment

The use of expert judgment is another issue that was the subject of considerable controversy during the review of the first draft of NUREG–1150. Serious criticisms of the methods used in the first draft to obtain these judgments led the staff and its contractors to implement more formal and rigorous methods. The committees reviewing the second draft had a number of general comments on the use of expert judgment. These included:

● "The formal methods that NUREG–1150 employed for such elicitation and the extensive debates that have ensued constitute a significant advance in PSA methodology, since they force visibility on the use of 'engineering judgment,' which is abundant, yet often hidden, in safety studies. The critical element of the whole process, e.g., the selection of the experts, is now widely recognized and appreciated." (Kouts 4.7)

● "Expert opinion elicitation is technically less satisfying than the use of detailed, validated analytical procedures, or experimental data. Considering the lack of understanding of some phenomena, the uncertainties in the scenarios, and the state of development of many of the analytical procedures, some form of expert opinion was unavoidable, however." (Kouts 4.4) (The committee then continued with a set of more specific comments, some of which are appropriate for staff response. These are discussed below.)

● "It can be hoped that, in the long term, the accumulation of experience will help to narrow the distributions in many inputs and outputs of risk assessments. This is, however, unlikely for many of the important ones, because the objective of safety is specifically to avoid just those events that would generate the data useful for risk analysis." (Kouts 4.11.2)

● "There is a general agreement that the techniques used for eliciting expert opinion in preparation of the second draft were significantly better than those used for the first draft. However, with insufficient information there can be no experts. Thus, use of the term 'expert opinion' in a description of some of the Level 2 work may be misleading. We applaud efforts to improve on the Level 2 treatment of previous PRAs. We nevertheless believe that the results from Level 2 presented in this latest [second] draft must be regarded as having major uncertainties in both calculated mean values and in estimated uncertainties." (ACRS)

More specific comments by the review committees are itemized below and staff responses provided.

Comment: Formal, professionally structured expert opinion is preferable to the current alternative, according to which the individual PRA analysts make informal judgments that are not always well documented. However, it is not as technically defensible as analysis using detailed, validated codes. The reproducibility of expert opinion results is a concern (Kouts 4.4).

Response:

The staff agrees that a PRA will be improved by having as many robust calculations as possible. However, it should be noted that it will also never be possible to remove expert judgment from a PRA. A PRA is a procedure for assembling information from many sources, including experimental data, theoretical calculations, and mechanistic code calculations, some of which are conflicting and incomplete. The process of obtaining expert opinions such as used in NUREG–1150 provides a way to review this information and put it in a form that is suitable for use in a PRA. The outcome of this process will always be improved by better information, including calculations by detailed, validated codes. However, some type of expert judgment is always associated with the use of code calculations for several reasons. First, a code calculation is performed for a very specific accident, but the results of this calculation are used in a PRA for groups of "similar" accidents. This type of aggregation requires judgment since the performance of a calculation for every possible accident is not feasible. Second, it is not possible to fully "validate" the mechanistic codes that are used in reactor accident calculations. Thus, there is always a judgment that must be made with respect to the acceptability of a code calculation for a specific application. Third, judgments with respect to model formulation and model parameters must be made to use a code. Thus, the opinion of this "expert" will always enter into the calculations and results.

In the NUREG–1150 uses of expert judgments, two factors acted to reduce the potential impact of this concern: the information being obtained from experts was in the form of probability distributions rather than single or best estimates; and, for key issues, a diversity of judgments was sought. Nonetheless, the staff agrees that the reproducibility of expert judgments can be of concern and expects to support research in this area in the future.

Comment: There is always a question as to "who is an expert on a given issue." The membership of expert panels for the second draft of NUREG–1150 seemed to be better than for the first draft. Yet it still seemed to be unbalanced in that panels still contained more analysts and fewer persons with practical engineering experience who might have expertise on the phenomena; the panels included more users and fewer generators of data than is preferable (Kouts 4.4, 7.2; ACRS).

Response:

The method used to select the members of the expert panels for the NUREG–1150 risk analyses is discussed in Reference E.24. As described there, one goal was to select experts with a diversity of backgrounds. However, experts familiar with reactor safety were usually selected for practical purposes. That is, the project schedule did not permit the time, in general, to educate experts in very specialized areas in the more general area of reactor safety. Two experts on specific phenomena with no familiarity with reactor safety analysis were selected: one on the source term panel and one on the containment loadings panel. One of the experts felt uncomfortable extrapolating his knowledge to reactor accident sequences and declined to continue participation. The second expert went through the effort to educate himself on reactor risk and provided valuable input.

Comment: Expert opinion may have been relied upon too heavily in some instances. An important example is the treatment of core cooling after containment failure. In this case, expert opinion was used to argue that equipment would fail 70–80 percent of the time if environmental temperatures exceeded equipment qualification limits. No explicit analysis was performed to determine the impact of local environmental conditions on equipment heatup and the potential for subsequent failure. It may have been thought that the analysis would have been too time-consuming. It would have been appropriate if possible to have developed these analyses and then to have subjected them to critical review to which expert opinion could have been directed (Kouts 4.4).

Response:

The staff and its contractors did obtain additional information and perform extensive analyses to eliminate the need for or support expert judgments and to supplement the information available in the literature. For the specific issue cited, the experts did receive, for example, information on equipment tolerances and lubricant breakdown temperatures. More generally, many calculations were commissioned specifically for the NUREG–1150 study and presented to the expert panels for review. Some examples of code calculations commissioned include those performed with CONTAIN, CORCON, the Source Term Code

Package, MELCOR, and MELPROG. Such calculations were performed for specific issues and are described in Reference E.16.

Comment: There are some subjects for which the expert opinions were either incomplete or were not targeted on the correct issue because definition of the issue evolved subsequent to the elicitation process and resources were lacking to update it. In these cases, the Sandia staff modified the expert opinion in order to treat the redefined issue. Unfortunately, these new calculations were not reviewed with the expert panel and are not reported in the NUREG-1150 main report or other documentation available to the Kouts committee (Kouts 4.4).

Response:

There were issues in which the responses of the experts were used in a slightly different context than was originally intended. There were two reasons for this:

- The experts had different perceptions of the question asked of them; thus, the information was received from the individual experts in different formats. To aggregate these issues, it was necessary to extrapolate and interpolate some of the expert responses.

- The definition of the issue sometimes evolved subsequent to the elicitation process. In some cases, the issue was much more complex than was anticipated at the time of the elicitation; an example is the treatment of multiple containment failure modes during fast pressure rises. In these cases, the information from the expert panels was reformatted or extrapolated in order to aggregate the response.

In all cases, the original elicitation notes for the accident progression issues and the source term issues have been documented (after review by the experts) in Reference E.16. Any manipulations that were performed on the expert elicitation are described in a section that preceded the individual expert issue documentation, entitled "Method of Aggregation." In virtually all cases, the manipulations were discussed with the experts prior to its use to ensure that the information was not misused.

Comment: The study assigned equal weight factors to the opinions of all experts. Other methods that can develop unequal weight factors were not used (Kouts 4.4).

Response:

The staff and its contractors considered a variety of methods of combining expert judgments, including methods using unequal weighting factors. As noted in Appendix A, the method of equal weighting was chosen because this simple method has been found in many studies (e.g., Ref. E.23) to perform the best.

Comment: The ACRS was told that the budget for the study provided only enough funding to support the participation of about 20 percent of the experts who served on the panels. The remainder were drawn from the NRC staff or from organizations with contractual relationships to the NRC. This biased the selection toward people whose organizations depend upon the NRC for support (ACRS).

Response:

Roughly 30 percent of the experts were funded directly by the NUREG-1150 study. However, the remainder of the experts were supported by two groups: the NRC and the nuclear industry (e.g., EPRI). Overall, approximately 30 percent of the experts were supported directly by the NUREG-1150 study, 45 percent by other NRC projects, and 25 percent by the nuclear industry.

Comment: The expert opinion procedure is complex, time-consuming, and expensive. Therefore, the full scope of the methodology may have very limited future application. It is unlikely that an expert opinion procedure of this magnitude will be repeated for several years, although expert elicitation on single or narrow issues may be practical. However, it should be remembered that throughout the study analysts had to decide how to use technical information of all kinds; this "expert judgment" is necessary in all PRAs (Kouts 4.4; ACRS).

Response:

The staff agrees that the expert judgment methods used in NUREG–1150 may have limited utility in future work because of the time and cost involved. The staff intends to pursue research in this area with the intent of making the formal uses of expert judgments and the performance of quantitative uncertainty analyses more practical.

Comment: The discussion of issue quantification could be substantially improved, with much clearer indication of what probability distributions were developed by the staff and which specific issues were quantified by the expert review panels (Kouts 7.3; ANS 2.a.8.a).

Response:

The staff agrees with this comment. A table indicating what variables were included in the uncertainty study for the Surry plant (Ref. E.12), and how they were quantified (by expert panels, by NUREG–1150 staff, or by user function), is provided as an example in Section C.1 of Appendix C. Similar tables for the other four plants are provided in References E.13 and E.26 through E.28.

E.5 Accident Frequency Analysis

The review committees and the ACRS had a number of general and specific comments on the accident frequency analysis performed in the NUREG–1150 project. These comments are itemized below, beginning with the subject receiving the most comment, human reliability analysis, discussed in Section E.5.1. Section E.5.2 then provides a discussion of comments on external-event analysis, and Section E.5.3 provides a discussion of other comments on the accident frequency analysis.

E.5.1 Human Reliability Analysis

The Kouts committee provided considerable comment on the subject of human reliability analysis (HRA). As a general comment, the committee noted that:

- "Given the current state of the art in HRA, it would be unreasonable to expect NUREG–1150 to resolve all the outstanding issues including use of a universally accepted model." (Kouts 4.8.2)

The ACRS also provided a general comment on this subject:

- "As other reviewers have reported, there are recognized deficiencies in the state-of-the-art treatments of human performance; and this report is not free of these deficiencies."

In addition, a number of specific comments were provided. These are itemized below along with staff responses.

Comment: NUREG–1150 pioneered the explicit treatment of model uncertainties and the use of expert panels to weigh the relative merits of alternative methods of analysis, but such an approach was not been employed for human actions such as errors of commission and complex situations in control rooms such as in the early phases of an BWR ATWS accident (Kouts 4.8.2).

Response:

The staff agrees that the human reliability analysis should have been performed in a manner more consistent with the remainder of the risk analyses.

Human reliability analysis has been the subject of extensive research in the past few years and has led to the development and initial application of techniques to deal with such issues as human errors of commission. NRC continues to perform a substantial amount of research in HRA, as described in Reference E.8. The demonstration and more widespread use of improved HRA methods in PRA is planned to be the subject of future work by NRC.

Comment: It would have been valuable if the theoretical HRAs of the ATWS sequences had been tested against analysis of real events as a basis for an in-depth analysis of uncertainties in HRA. This could be done as part of expert opinion input on the merits of different HRA models. Such an approach to the

ATWS HRA appears more appropriate and consistent with the use of expert panels in the remainder of NUREG–1150 (Kouts 4.8.4, 7.2).

Response:

The validation of human reliability models (by comparisons with actual events, simulator exercises, etc.) is an integral part of the present NRC program in HRA (Ref. E.8). Future NRC PRA work will make use of such models and thus should provide a better assessment of human performance and its importance to risk.

Comment: For NUREG–1150, the argument was advanced that the conservative screening procedures that have been employed and the wide uncertainty ranges that have been assigned to human error rates have the effect of including the results that other models would have generated. However, such an approach goes against the presumed goal of a PRA, namely, the realistic estimation of risks. Furthermore, the use of an error factor does not necessarily cover the possibility that the models systematically overestimate or underestimate the human error rates (Kouts 4.8.2).

Response:

Conservative screening values were used in the initial quantification of human error probabilities. However, for those events that were potentially significant contributors to core damage frequency, more detailed analyses were performed (this approach being designed to expend significant resources only on those events that are most important). Different types of probability distributions, such as maximum entropy or lognormal, were assigned as appropriate. It is possible that the mean values produced in the analyses could be systematically high or low because of various types of systematic errors. However, the uncertainty analysis did account for these errors in the sense that many of the human error uncertainty distributions were correlated. That is, when a value near the high end of the distribution was chosen for one variable, then a value near the high end of the distribution was chosen for all similar human errors. Thus, the variability did account somewhat for systematic errors. This approach, coupled with the fact that very wide uncertainty distributions were applied to these variables, leads the staff to believe that the treatment of human error uncertainties was adequate for the types of actions included within the scope of the study, recognizing the state of technology of HRA at the time when the work was performed. As noted above, the NRC is currently funding considerable research in the area of HRA (Ref. E.8).

Comment: Considering the different Grand Gulf and Peach Bottom analyses of operator failure to initiate the standby liquid control system during an ATWS event, it is unclear to what extent the differences in estimated probabilities is due to the different methods employed and to the different groups of analysts that have implemented them. It may be questioned if the relatively simple methods used are the most appropriate for very complex, high-stress situations (Kouts 4.8.4).

Response:

The HRA methods used for the Grand Gulf and Peach Bottom ATWS analyses included a detailed task analysis, using the THERP method (Ref. E.29) for Grand Gulf and the SLIM-MAUD method (Ref. E.30) for Peach Bottom. The staff acknowledges that use of different methods and analysts can have an impact on the results obtained and that the impact on the two plant ATWS studies of these differences cannot be easily estimated.

While the use of different analysts can influence the results, it should be recognized that plant design differences were found to be important in NUREG–1150. With respect to ATWS accident sequences in Grand Gulf and Peach Bottom, several such important design differences exist. For example, the standby liquid control system in Grand Gulf is designed to inject boron via the high-pressure core spray sparger, while in Peach Bottom boron is injected into the bottom of the reactor vessel. This difference leads to differences in timing of ATWS events and the procedures established by the plants (operator actions to lower and raise water levels required at Peach Bottom are not needed in Grand Gulf).

Comment: It is beyond the capabilities of present PRA models to account for the influence of management quality on risk; thus it is understandable that NUREG–1150 does not address these issues. While management quality may not be quantifiable in PRA in the near future, its impact on safety is currently being addressed through other NRC and INPO [Institute of Nuclear Power Operations] work. It is important to bear in mind that management quality is not reflected in the risk information as results and perspectives are used (Kouts 4.9).

Response:

Such influences have not been included in NUREG-1150 (or in any other PRA). The present NRC human factors research program (Ref. E.8) includes the study of organizational and management influences on plant safety, including consideration of how such influences can be accounted for in risk studies such as NUREG-1150. Completion of this research should provide some perspective on the degree to which these influences can be incorporated.

Comment: The inclusion of some recovery actions was state of the art. However, the assumptions behind actual recovery curves are not always clear (Kouts 3.2.1.7).

Response:

The recovery analysis included an evaluation of both the time available for recovery and the probability of the operator correctly performing the task. For some faults, actual historical data exist. For example, data exist for all electrical-type faults (i.e., offsite power and diesel generator faults) and faults associated with the power conversion system. For other type faults, historical data did not exist. This recovery information is documented in Reference E.31. For these situations, an HRA or recovery analysis was performed to determine the probability of failure to recover. These recovery curves and "generic" human behavior curves are obtained directly from use of the THERP method (Ref. E.29).

Comment: Innovative recovery actions not covered by operating or emergency procedures should not be included in the baseline analysis, but should be reserved for potential reductions in risk (Kouts 3.2.1.7).

Response:

For some of the accidents analyzed in NUREG-1150, several hours pass before the onset of core damage. In severe accidents of such time duration, an emergency response team would be involved to support the operating crew. It would, therefore, be unrealistic not to allow any innovative recovery actions, considering that such options would be under active investigation and consideration. For these reasons, and recognizing the goal of performing realistic analyses in PRA, credit for innovative recovery in such accidents was permitted in the NUREG-1150 analyses.

It should be noted that, while permitted, very few innovative actions were ultimately incorporated into the analyses. Although several innovative recovery actions were proposed, some of these were incorporated into plant procedures (by the licensee), while others were found to be unnecessary for further analysis because of the already low estimated frequency of the associated accident sequences or the low probability of success.

Comment: Special attention should be given to further development of human reliability analysis, and to proper calibration of the procedures used for it, to enable comparisons to be made between plants and quantitative safety goals (Kouts 4.12, 7.3).

Response:

As discussed in the responses to a number of the previous comments, the NRC has a significant research program under way in the area of human reliability analysis (Ref. E.8).

E.5.2 External-Event Analysis

Specific Comments

Comment: A simplified approach was taken in NUREG-1150 in defining seismic initiators, which leads to failure from all resulting transients, small or large (Kouts 4.3.2).

Response:

All seismically induced transients were not assumed to result in "failure." It is assumed in the analysis that an earthquake will lead to at least one initiator that will require the plant to shut down (either automatically or as a result of operator action).

The occurrence of any of these initiating events, however, does not necessarily imply that core damage will occur. Given that such an initiating event occurs, the same (event tree and fault tree) process is used to assess the conditional probability of core damage as was performed for the internal-event analyses. System failure probabilities may be higher because of earthquake-induced damage, but they are not assumed to be of unity probability.

Comment: Although plant experience was used to establish fire initiation frequencies, judgmental factors were used to determine whether a fire, once started, would persist and cause damage in spite of fire mitigation systems and actions. It would seem that the same data base that was used for fire initiation could and should have been used to give a more realistic value for fire persistence (ANS 3.f.3.a).

Response:

Credit was taken for fire mitigation systems, both manual and automatic, in each fire scenario where applicable. In the case of manual suppression, the same fire data base used to develop the fire initiation frequencies was also used to develop a probability of suppression in any given time frame. For automatic suppression systems, several other studies were used to determine reliability values, as these could not be determined directly from the fire occurrence data base. The data indicated that, for fires in critical locations, the fire was always eventually suppressed (either automatically or manually) but seldom before damage to critical equipment would be predicted to occur (using the COMPBRN model of fire propagation (Ref. E.32)).

Comment: Research in seismic modeling is warranted with the objective of improving the basic model for prediction of attenuation and ground motion and for developing a consensus of the use of one model or model set based as much as practicable on region-specific spectral shapes. Effort should also be made to improve the basic model to reflect greater source depths and regional variations with the appropriate reflections of substrata waves (Kouts 7.3).

Response:

NRC and others continue to sponsor research to improve the general understanding of seismic hazard, including the areas noted above. Such work is described in Reference E.33.

E.5.3 Other Accident Frequency Comments

In addition to the comments itemized above on human reliability and external-event analyses, the committees had a number of other comments on the NUREG-1150 accident frequency analysis. Some general comments provided by the committees included:

- "[The plant damage state analysis] was more detailed than the corresponding analysis in other recent PSA's. It provided an efficient interface with the detailed and complex accident progression and containment loads analysis, and constitutes an advance in PSA methodology." (Kouts 3.2.1.8)

- "In respect to including the modes of containment failure, and in the level of detail, the [accident sequence event tree] analysis was advanced other than typically seen in Level 1 PSA's performed at the time of the NUREG-1150 analysis." (Kouts 3.2.1.2)

- "Although NUREG-1150 is described as being 'a set of modern PRAs, having the limitations of all such studies,' the level of modeling in the accident frequency analysis is not as detailed in some areas as that found in other current PRAs." (ANS 2.a.8.b)

- "A rigorous analysis would always combine the generic and plant-specific [failure data] information. In fact, this is often done using Bayes' theorem. However, we note that in general the numerical differences between the approximate methods of NUREG-1150 and the rigorous approach are insignificant." (Kouts 3.2.1.6)

More specific comments made by the committees are itemized below and staff responses provided.

Comment: Since the first draft was issued, considerable effort was devoted to making the accident frequency analysis more robust. However, the NRC staff recognizes that the state of the art with respect to common-cause failures and human reliability analysis is imperfect and that further improvements can be made in these crucial areas. These areas have not been treated as top-level issues in the expert elicitation process (Kouts 6.3).

Response:

Common-cause failures and selected human error probabilities were offered to the accident frequency analysis panel as issues. The panel concluded that the approach being taken by the analysis team for common-cause failures was appropriate and that expert judgment would not significantly improve the process. Human errors could not be readily considered as a single issue because each action being considered was unique, requiring a separate analysis. The panel did consider several specific human error issues considered to be particularly important. In addition, sensitivity studies on the importance of human error were performed, as discussed in Appendix C.

Comment: The consideration of operating experience in the so-called subtle interactions, represents a good attempt to ensure completeness of failure modes. The method of treatment of dependent failures was state of the art in most respects. The documentation of common-cause failure analysis is difficult to follow. For example, in some instances references were made to EPRI common-cause methods and data, but it appears that in reality a modified beta-factor method was used, which was itself state of the art. The probability of failure of all station batteries is critical to the final results and therefore necessitates better substantiation. Recovery from common-cause failure was restricted to selected electrical equipment (Kouts 3.2.1.4).

Response:

Common-cause failures are discussed in Appendix C and in Reference E.31. The common-cause analysis used in the NUREG–1150 analyses was based primarily on EPRI methods and data. EPRI generic component beta factors were used in the calculation of the common-cause failure (CCF) rates. The CCF rates were calculated as follows:

$$CCF = Q * \beta_n$$

where

Q = Total failure rate

β_n = Beta factor for n components.

For some components, there was not a generic component beta factor for the number of components modeled. In these cases, the EPRI beta factor was modified. In addition, for some components (e.g., batteries, air-operated valves), there were no EPRI generic component beta factors. For these components, other sources or methods were used to calculate the beta factor.

Common-cause failures of the batteries were analyzed in detail in other studies (Ref. E.34) and were used in the NUREG–1150 analysis. Recovery credit for common-cause failures was included where data existed.

Comment: In the analysis of loss of feedwater initiating events, it was assumed that condensate would also be lost, thereby eliminating a potential source of injection capability. For such an initiating event, the recovery potential may be underestimated because of this assumption (Kouts 3.2.1.1).

Response:

The loss of feedwater (LOFW) was treated on a plant-specific basis. For Grand Gulf, upon examination of LOFW, it was determined that condensate would not be lost. For Peach Bottom, it was assumed that condensate was lost with LOFW; however, credit was given for the recovery of the power conversion system, which included recovery of condensate. For PWRs, loss of condensate was included as one of the contributors to LOFW. However, because the LOFW initiating event was not an important contributor to the estimated core damage frequency, no credit for recovery of condensate was considered necessary nor given.

Comment: In general, it appears that very little plant-specific thermal-hydraulic analysis was conducted. Instead, the analysts relied on the results of generic analyses and made judgments as to the degree of applicability in many scenarios (Kouts 3.2.1.2).

Response:

When necessary, plant-specific thermal-hydraulic calculations were performed (e.g., BWR ATWS sequences, ice condenser containment spray actuation timing, and boiloff calculations). Additional thermal-hydraulic calculations were not deemed necessary because a large library of calculations already existed, including those from NRC research programs, vendor analyses, and other industry programs. In addition, actual plant experience was used. For example, the thermal-hydraulic response to a steam generator tube rupture was based in part upon the data from the North Anna tube rupture incident.

Comment: Some success criteria may be too conservative, e.g., both PORVs are assumed to be required for feed and bleed in PWRs (Kouts 3.2.1.2).

Response:

As much as possible, success criteria were developed to be realistic, as opposed to conservative. For example, low-pressure systems were allowed to lead to success in BWR ATWS sequences, including loss of the standby liquid control system, whereas previous studies might not have considered that possibility. In some cases, the success of a particular system was questionable based on information available in the time frame of the study. In these cases, conservative choices were made. Plant procedures (e.g., those that called for both PORVs to be opened in the case of feed and bleed cooling) were also influential in the decisions made in such cases.

Comment: The Grand Gulf ATWS analysis included the two event tree branches of early and late closure of the main steam isolation valves. In the Peach Bottom ATWS analysis, it was, probably conservatively, assumed that the main steam isolation valves (MSIVs) closed for all scenarios. We have found no justification for this difference based on design data or plant operating experience (Kouts 3.2.1.3).

Response:

A plant-specific analysis of MSIV response during ATWS was performed for both Grand Gulf and Peach Bottom. It was not assumed in the Peach Bottom ATWS analysis that all scenarios resulted in MSIV closure. Based on a detailed analysis, it was concluded that all ATWS sequences (with MSIVs open) would lead to isolation signals to the MSIVs.

Comment: Electrical control and actuation circuits were not included in the common-cause failure analysis (Kouts 3.2.1.4).

Response:

Electrical control and actuation circuits faults were included as part of the component random failure rate. The same applies for the common-cause failures. The faults comprising the common-cause failures for components (i.e., valves, pumps, diesels, etc.) were dominated by electrical control and actuation circuit faults.

Comment: Expert judgments assign large uncertainty to the issue of reactor coolant pump seal failure, which is actually susceptible to experimental determination. It is not readily apparent how the bimodal distribution of NUREG-1150 would be affected by the revised estimates of leakage rates and times for initiation of leakage (Kouts 4.6.2).

More recent information and the development of some new reactor coolant pump seal designs since the NUREG-1150 risk studies were completed would lead to a prediction of risk less than that reported (ACRS).

Response:

The expert judgment process was intended to characterize the current understanding of the issue rather than provide resolution. The information base used by the experts included data from experimental programs by Westinghouse, by NRC, and in France. (Appendix C now includes a section of how this issue was addressed; a detailed description is provided in Ref. E.15.)

It should also be noted that the expert judgment process considered the potential importance of the new Westinghouse seal design (not yet in place in the plants analyzed). The experts concluded that seal failure with the new seals would be very unlikely. This would have two effects on the NUREG-1150 analyses. First, the core damage frequency would be reduced because more recovery time would be available prior to core damage. However, for those accident sequences that continue on to core damage, the core damage may occur with the reactor coolant system at high pressure, leading to high containment building loadings at time of reactor vessel breach.

Comment: It is likely that the performance of relief valves, which must function if the feed and bleed operation is to be successful, is not well represented by the data for valve performance used in the NUREG-1150 calculations (ACRS).

Response:

The staff agrees that there is now operating experience data that suggest that the PORV failure rates are optimistic. However, since failure of the feed and bleed function is assessed to be dominated by human errors (to actuate the system), it does not appear that increased failure rates for the PORVs would significantly affect the likelihood of failure to feed and bleed.

Comment: There is now a significant body of evidence to indicate that the failure probability used to describe the operation of certain key motor-operated valves is too low. This may have an important bearing on the outcome of several accident sequences described in the report (ACRS).

Response:

The staff agrees that there is now evidence that motor-operated valve failure rates are, under some conditions, higher than those used in NUREG-1150. The NUREG-1150 analyses have not been reevaluated in detail to assess the potential impact of the newer failure rates. It is the staff's judgment that, while the impact would be noticeable, it would not be dominating.

Comment: Plant-specific information is becoming increasingly important in PRA; such information should be collected and placed on file for future use (Kouts 7.3).

Response:

The NRC has developed a data base for the accident frequency analysis models developed in NUREG-1150 (and for other PRAs as well). This data base can be accessed via two computer codes, SARA and IRRAS (Refs. E.35 and E.36), which permit the manipulation of the data for sensitivity analyses, etc. These codes and the data base have been installed and are seeing use in several locations at NRC (and its contractors).

In 1990, the NRC initiated work to assess the feasibility of developing a similar data base and acquisition/analysis system for the accident progression, source term, and risk analysis models of NUREG-1150. This system would make use of data generated with the detailed NUREG-1150 codes, such as EVNTRE (Ref. E.37) and PRAMIS (Ref. E.38).

Comment: The NUREG-1150 documentation does not allow a reviewer to determine how particular events contributed to the frequency of loss of offsite power and subsequent recovery (Kouts 3.2.1.1).

Response:

As noted in the report, NUREG-1150 provides a summary of the methods and results of the five PRAs performed. More detailed information is contained in the underlying contractor reports (Refs. E.15 through E.21, E.12, E.13, and E.26 through E.28). Even these, however, do not contain some of the raw data used to develop and quantify the risk models. Such data are retained in the project files. Included in these files are the data on specific losses of offsite power and its recovery. These data included all events at U.S. nuclear power plants through 1987. These included plant-centered, grid, and weather-related faults. Particular events that could not occur at a particular site were eliminated from the data base for that plant. Further, the analysis considered the operating history at each plant. Plant-specific recovery curves were then generated based on an aggregate of all loss of offsite power events, as opposed to separate recovery curves for each type of failure event.

E.6 Accident Progression Analysis

The review committees had a number of specific comments on the NUREG–1150 accident progression analysis, the most important of which appears to relate to the level of detail in the analysis, compared with the detailed accident phenomenogical computer codes and with the present level of understanding of accident phenomenology. These specific comments are itemized below and staff responses provided. Comments dealing with the closely related subject of accident source term methods are discussed in Section E.7.

Comment: The level of detail in the accident progression analysis appears to have exceeded the understanding of the phenomena involved. It implied greater insight into the processes assumed to be taking place than was justified (Kouts 3.2.2.1, 7.2; ACRS).

If phenomenological models are not provided and directly used, the dependence of the results of the accident progression analysis on governing physical phenomena is hidden (Kouts 3.2.2.1, 7.2).

The generality of the structure of trees and the flexibility to use different levels of modeling capability and details to answer the questions at branch points make the method very powerful, but concern can arise about the meaningfulness of computed results if little information is available about the issues. The possibility of introducing high-level issues makes the method efficient, but this feature should be used with caution if applied to issues with a weak information basis (Kouts 3.2.2.1, 7.2).

We note that in the back end subjective distributions are given for high-level parameters ("issues") that describe the outcomes of complex physical or chemical processes whose basic uncertainties are at lower levels. Mechanistic computational models that would relate these lower-level parameters to the higher-level issues are not employed (for example, the amount of core debris involved in ex-vessel steam explosion is an issue, and its dependence on such lower-level parameters as heat generation rates and chemical reaction rates is not modeled explicitly). Developing subjective probability distributions for high-level parameters may not always be the best approach since the physics of the underlying processes does not get the attention that would be desirable (Kouts 4.7).

Response:

The comments first question whether the detail exceeds the state of knowledge. The staff does not believe so. The intended use of a study to some extent defines the appropriate level of detail. The level of detail was chosen to pass the appropriate information on to the source term analysis and to allow the variation of parameters in the integrated uncertainty analysis. In order to meet these two objectives, it was necessary to form the probabilistic models with high-level issues. Uncertain responses to the high-level issues resulted in wide uncertainty distributions. The use of wide uncertainty distributions to characterize processes that are not well understood should not imply greater insight into the process than is justified but should highlight the uncertainty of that process.

The information presented in NUREG–1150 provides insight into the importance of the high-level parameters and not the governing physical phenomena (e.g., chemical reaction rates). Also, the accident progression event trees used to model the accident progression are based on these high-level parameters. To evaluate the branch point probabilities, however, the high-level parameters are decomposed to the level of the governing physical phenomena (as documented in Ref. E.16).

Because of the complexity of the accident progression, it would have been computationally impossible to model the accident framework for each accident sequence at the physical process level (heat transfer correlations, oxidation rates, etc.). To obtain the insights necessary on the underlying physical processes, it is necessary to establish what high-level parameters are important and then refer to the copious documentation provided on parameter distribution development in Reference E.16.

The staff agrees with the comment that the user should interpret the results of the study carefully when there is a weak information base associated with high-level issues. The NUREG–1150 approach was to include these issues in our models and apply appropriate uncertainty bounds to the parameter distributions.

Comment: There is inconsistency in the detail of the accident progression analysis. This is in part because the state of knowledge with respect to severe accident phenomenology in BWRs versus PWRs is different, the use of expert elicitation for severe accident issues was not the same for all plants, and there was a large uncertainty in operator behavior with respect to post-core-damage recovery actions (Kouts 6.3).

Response:

The general process for performing the accident progression analysis was consistent between PWRs and BWRs. The BWR accident progression event trees (APETs) tended to be larger and more complex because there are more interactions between the containment and the reactor coolant system in BWRs and because the failure location in BWR containments can have a large impact on release fractions. The quality of the information available for input parameter distribution varied for the different issues because of the different amount of experimental and analytical studies performed, but was not clearly superior for either BWRs or PWRs.

There are some issues that have been studied more extensively for PWRs (in-vessel melt progression, direct containment heating). This may have resulted in some inconsistency in the quality of the response on some issues, but the selection criteria for the expert elicitation issues were applied consistently to all plants analyzed.

Comment: The bin "no vessel breach" has a relatively high conditional probability for all plant damage states of PWRs. Yet, the capability to model the issue of core degradation before vessel breach is rather poor. We are unable at present to judge the validity of the conditional probabilities associated with this accident progression bin (Kouts 4.6.1).

Response:

The staff agrees that there are considerable uncertainties associated with this issue. However, it is felt that the approaches used in this study adequately represent the knowledge base as it pertains to this issue. The approach used in the NUREG–1150 analyses is described in Part 6 of Reference E.16.

Comment: Only one of the three experts whose opinions were elicited provided a distribution function for temperature-induced hot leg failure. The other two made the statements "...if necessary conditions for high temperature were met, the leg would always fail...," and "...if high temperatures lasted long enough hot leg would always fail. For shorter time at high temperature hot leg would sometimes fail..."

Since the crucial point in the analysis is the estimation of the hot leg temperature, we cannot see how the two cited statements were incorporated into the aggregated probability distribution presented in NUREG–1150. Therefore, we are unable to judge the validity of the result (Kouts 4.6.3).

Response:

The three experts that considered the temperature-induced hot leg failure all addressed the estimation of the hot leg temperature in their assessments. Two of the experts' decompositions of the issue established continuous distributions for failure probability, the other decomposition provided a point estimate. Each decomposition of the issue was different, yet all addressed hot leg temperatures.

There were many cases in which the distributions (and the associated rationales) provided by experts on the same issue differed significantly. For example, one expert might have felt that the uncertainty in an issue was primarily stochastic in nature while another expert might have felt that the uncertainty was entirely the result of the lack of understanding of the physical process. The method of aggregating distributions (described in Ref. E.16) accommodated different perceptions of the results. Further information on the specific expert analysis of temperature-induced hot leg failure may be found in Part 1 of Reference E.16.

Comment: The treatment of the pressure rise at vessel breach as a single issue by the expert panel obscured a more complete understanding of how the various components contributed to the reduced probability of early containment failure (Kouts 4.6.4).

Response:

The containment loads expert panel felt that tightly coupled phenomena were responsible for the loads that accompany vessel failure. Furthermore, the experts felt that there were synergistic relationships among the various phenomena. Thus, because a simple relationship that ties together the various phenomena involved did not exist, the expert panel did not believe that these phenomena could be isolated without sacrificing the credibility of the final distribution (i.e., the load experienced by the containment). It was their opinion that artificially breaking apart the loads would not provide a realistic picture of the events that are taking place.

The phenomena that contribute to the loads at vessel breach and the importance of the various phenomena for a given distribution are discussed in Reference E.16. From the descriptions of the experts' rationales, the importance of various events to the loads at vessel breach can be obtained. Discussion of the reasons for which these loads are less important now than in the first draft of NUREG–1150 is provided in Section C.5 of Appendix C.

Comment: We note that the concrete erosion progresses faster and with greater intensity than is estimated in NUREG–1150, with a corresponding influence on hydrogen production. However, we agree with the assessment in NUREG–1150 that the meltthrough per se introduces no important influence on health risk (Kouts 4.6.5).

For reasons explained in the section on basemat meltthrough, we believe that this process (MCCI) [molten core-concrete interactions] is modeled incorrectly, with the consequence that the hydrogen generation rate in the ex-vessel phase of accidents in PWRs would be underestimated (Kouts 4.6.6).

Response:

The hydrogen generation rate during core-concrete interactions was based on calculations with the COR-CON computer code, as discussed in Reference E.16. The amount of hydrogen produced in the core-concrete interaction phase is dependent on how much unoxidized metal is available, which in turn is dependent on how much has been oxidized in prior phases. From the CORCON calculations, it appears that most of the unoxidized metals remaining in the debris as core-concrete interactions begin are oxidized rapidly. The staff therefore believes that most release rates predicted by current techniques and considering experimental evidence are bounded by the range of release rates in NUREG–1150, when considering in-vessel hydrogen production rate, the at-vessel-breach hydrogen release rate, and the early core-concrete interaction hydrogen production rate.

Because early containment failures and containment bypass accidents tended to dominate the risk, and because there was already so much hydrogen in the containment at the beginning of core-concrete interaction, the amount of hydrogen produced during core-concrete interaction was not considered to be highly risk significant and thus was not varied in the overall uncertainty analysis. As such, while an estimate of hydrogen production based on CORCON calculations may not agree closely with all estimates from experiments such as those performed in the BETA facility, such differences are not believed to be important to the overall risk estimates.

Comment: A separate accident progression bin should be used for basemat meltthrough because knowledge of the consequences of this form of release, though not important from the standpoint of damage to the public, is useful for other purposes (Kouts 3.2.2.3).

Response:

The accident progression results that are shown in NUREG–1150 are summary accident progression bins, grouped together for presentation purposes only. It is possible to separate the basemat meltthrough event from the long-term containment failure event when presenting results of the detailed accident progression analysis. However, in the source term analysis, the two events were binned together. Thus it is not possible to extract separate source term and consequence results for the basemat meltthrough and late containment failure events without performing new calculations. This was not done in the NUREG–1150 analyses because of the low estimated risk significance of both of these failure mechanisms.

Comment: The lack of information about many of the physical phenomena that determine the performance of a containment system in a severe accident situation is such that only educated guesses can be made for some sequences that might make significant contributions to risk. Some important phenomenological issues (e.g., direct containment heating, Mark I shell meltthrough) were characterized quite differently in the first and second drafts even though there was not a major change in the information base. Further, no consideration was found on the impact of ex–vessel steam explosions on early containment failure. There is little unambiguous guidance here for a licensee performing an IPE (ACRS).

Response:

While the staff believes that significant progress has been made in the understanding of severe accident phenomenology, it also agrees that there is a need for more information on a number of specific issues, such as those highlighted by the ACRS. The staff recognized this in developing the guidance for licensee individual plant examinations (IPEs). Appendix 1 to the IPE generic letter (Ref. E.39) provides guidance on how licensees should deal with this lack of information.

It is correct that a number of phenomenological issues were characterized quite differently in the first and second draft versions of NUREG–1150. This reflects a greater information base on a number of important issues such as direct containment heating. The technical bases used by expert panels to assess such issues are discussed in considerable detail in Reference E.16.

The consideration of ex–vessel steam explosions is discussed in Section C.9 of NUREG–1150. This phenomenon was assessed to be of relatively minor importance in the five plants studied, in part because of the greater impacts of such issues as hydrogen combustion loads, etc. Its most prominent impact was in the Grand Gulf plant; Section 6.3 describes its importance relative to other phenomena.

Comment: The aggregate distribution for the probability of drywell shell meltthrough depends critically on the composition of the expert panel. Since this issue combines severe offsite consequences with very large uncertainties, a better resolution of the issues involved is clearly demanded (Kouts 4.6.7).

Response:

The staff agrees with the comment that a better resolution to the drywell shell meltthrough issue is advisable. This issue has been the subject of continuing research by NRC, as discussed in Reference E.40.

Comment: Large uncertainty contributions associated with some phenomena indicate the need for further research. These include the thermal-hydraulic phenomena associated with reactor coolant system (RCS) depressurization (as an accident management strategy), the ways in which the RCS may fail during high-pressure accident sequences in PWRs, and the assessment of threats to (and means to ensure the integrity of) the containment structure in case of a core meltdown resulting from pressure vessel failure (Kouts 7.3).

Response:

The staff agrees that the wide uncertainty distributions associated with specific phenomena provide one indication of where further research is desirable. Other considerations include the importance of the phenomena in question to risk (some wide uncertainty distributions may be acceptable if the contribution to risk is negligible) and the feasibility that further research will reduce the uncertainty bounds. All of these considerations are included by the staff when identifying and prioritizing future research.

Comment: Containment failure from seismic events was based on broad assumptions rather than structural analyses (Kouts 4.3.2).

Response:

Past work has shown that gross structural failure of a typical reinforced concrete containment due to earthquake motion is highly unlikely (Ref. E.41). Rather, it is the pipe penetrations that are most likely to fail because of the loads put on the penetrations by motion of the pipes passing through the penetrations. The loads most likely to cause penetration failure would arise from large motion or support failures of steam generators (in PWRs) or the reactor vessel (in BWRs). Hence, in the NUREG–1150 seismic analysis, containment failure was based on failure of the penetrations resulting from the failure of supports of the major reactor coolant system components. Since the vessel failure and the large LOCA initiating events included in the seismic analysis are based on support failures, it was assumed that some failure of the containment would occur, given either of these initiating events.

This assumption is based on a review of typical containment penetration configurations and discussion with structural experts and is based on the assumption that support failure would result in piping displacements of 1 to 2 feet, and that this would provide a sufficient load to fail the penetration. There are currently no data on the failure capacity of penetrations, given such loads. Hence, this assumption is based on engineering judgment.

In addition, estimates were needed on the size of the leak, given the failures described above. Again, based on typical penetration configurations, it was judged that the most likely crack size would be approximately 1/2 inch by 18 inches, similar to the small leak definition used in the rest of NUREG–1150. It was then assumed that a small leak would occur with a conditional probability of 0.9 and that a larger leak would occur with a conditional probability of 0.1. This assumption was based on the fact that piping supports inside containment would absorb a significant portion of the displacement-induced load and thus limit the leak size. Again, however, there are no data or calculations to substantiate this assumption.

E.7 Source Terms and Consequences

E.7.1 Source Terms

The Kouts committee had two general comments in the area of source term analysis. These were:

- "The overall strategy for generating the uncertainty values in Level 2, including the use of the XSOR codes, appears reasonable, since the tests that were made indicated that the uncertainties introduced by the codes are small compared to the overall Level 2 uncertainties." (Kouts 4.5)

- "Considerable caution is recommended in the use of the results obtained with the approximate XSOR codes without confirmation by more detailed codes." (Kouts 7.3)

The ANS committee had the following general comment:

- "The source terms reported in NUREG–1150 and the resultant offsite consequences should be considered as approximations, due to the reliance on the simplified mass balance XSOR models used to produce large numbers of source terms." (ANS 3.d.3)

In addition to these general comments, the review committees had a number of more specific comments. These are itemized below and staff responses provided.

Comment: The readers of NUREG–1150 should be aware that, of the thousands of source terms results presented, only a few were obtained using the detailed state-of-the-art calculational methods. The remainder were calculated using the parametric XSOR codes. This was a tradeoff to meet the need to generate many results in order to evaluate the uncertainties. The XSOR codes should be used with caution without confirmation by more detailed calculations (Kouts 7.3; ANS 2.a.8.d).

Response:

The XSOR codes were used for two reasons: (1) to generate source terms for the large number of accident progression bins identified in the accident progression analysis, and (2) to provide a means of incorporating the uncertainty in important analysis parameters into the integrated plant studies. Even if uncertainties were not being incorporated into the plant studies, it would be a very demanding undertaking to perform a mechanistic source term calculation for every accident progression bin. The alternative choices are assigning all accident progression bins to the results of a limited number of mechanistic calculations or attempting to modify the results of these calculations to more appropriately match the conditions associated with individual accident progression bins. The latter approach was chosen for the NUREG–1150 analyses.

The XSOR codes actually consist of three parts: a data base developed in the expert elicitation process, a mapping between the accident progression bins and this data base, and an algorithm for constructing source terms on the basis of individual accident progression bins and their associated data. In developing the data base, an attempt was made to use all available sources of information, including mechanistic code calculations, analytic solutions, and experimental data. Thus, the results of mechanistic calculations, as interpreted in the expert review process, are incorporated into the source terms generated by the XSOR codes.

Calculations were performed in which the SOR codes were benchmarked against a Source Term Code Package calculation for a specific scenario. The SOR code was then used to estimate the source terms for a similar scenario. The results compared favorably to a Source Term Code Package calculation made specifically for the second scenario (Ref. E.42).

Chapter 2 and Appendix A to NUREG–1150 have been modified to clarify the role of the XSOR codes.

Comment: Because of the approximate nature of the XSOR codes, the final version of NUREG–1150 should note the need for more exacting analysis of risk-significant accident sequences. The more detailed analysis should be performed and published in a supplement to NUREG–1150. This analysis should concentrate on best-estimate modeling and should be compared with the source terms in the final version of the report (Kouts 7.3; ANS 2.a.8.d).

Response:

The staff agrees with the comment. The staff intends to investigate the practicality of linking risk analysis calculations more closely to accident analysis codes such as MELCOR (Ref. E.43), potentially reducing the dependence on the XSOR codes. As noted below, the staff intends to initiate more detailed studies of the bypass accident sequences.

Comment: With respect to the containment bypass source term, it would be helpful to cite recent work (by EPRI) to help guide the reader to detailed assessments of some of the most important accidents identified in NUREG–1150. Citing more recent studies should help guide the users of NUREG–1150 to existing analyses that provide detailed assessments of some of the most important accident sequences identified in NUREG–1150 (Kouts 4.2.1).

The source terms for containment bypass accident sequences, including interfacing-system LOCAs and steam generator tube ruptures, were not the subject of detailed analyses and may be characterized as conservative approximations (ANS 2.a.8.d).

Response:

A number of Source Term Code Package computer analyses were performed to estimate the source terms for bypass accidents (Ref. E.44). Model development would be required, however, to more realistically treat certain aspects of such accident sequences as deposition in steam generators in a steam generator tube rupture-initiated core damage accident. The staff intends to perform more detailed studies of bypass sequences in followup work to NUREG–1150 and to compare the results of the new studies with those of NUREG–1150. More recent work by EPRI and others will be reflected in such followup comparisons.

Comment: A time cutoff of 24 hours after the onset of core degradation for the release of radionuclides was used throughout NUREG–1150, although no mention of this fact is contained in the report (ANS 2.a.8.d).

Response:

A time cutoff of 24 hours after the onset of core degradation was only used when considering the issue of late revolatilization from the reactor coolant system. Some of the members of the source term expert panel were concerned that the majority of the releases were going to occur extremely late in the accident (much later than 24 hours after the beginning of core damage). The project staff instructed the panel to consider late releases only up to 24 hours after core degradation. The reason for this was that some operator action to cool the reactor coolant system would be expected by that time (e.g., using external cooling by the containment sprays). The time cutoff was not an issue for the other source term processes that were considered because the majority of radionuclides were released well before 24 hours.

Appendix A has been modified to acknowledge this assumption.

Comment: The source terms and consequences of two classes of accidents, containment bypass and early containment failure, should be reported separately as well as the combined data presently displayed (ANS 2.b.9).

Response:

The plant-specific risk reports (Refs. E.12, E.13, and E.26 through E.28) present exceedance frequency curves for the source terms associated with different types of accidents, including containment bypass and early containment failure (e.g., see Figs. 3.3–4 and 3.3–9 in Ref. E.12). Equivalent information for consequences was not generated. However, the individual plant studies do present detailed information on the contribution of different accident types to risk.

Comment: It is not clear how credit is taken for radionuclide retention in the auxiliary building for PWR containment bypass accidents and the reactor building for BWR containment failures (ANS 5.e.4).

Response:

Two types of bypass accidents are considered in the PWR analyses: steam generator tube ruptures (SGTRs) and interfacing-system LOCAs (Event V). During an SGTR accident, the radionuclides are released directly to the environment; therefore, no radionuclide retention in the auxiliary building is considered. For the Event V accident, two methods for retention of radionuclides in the auxiliary (or safeguards) building are considered: retention associated with the building itself and retention from either water pools or water sprays. (At Surry, retention in the relatively small safeguards building is limited; however, there is the potential that the release will occur under a pool of water. At Sequoyah, the release could be mitigated by the fire spray system in the auxiliary building.)

Radionuclide retention in the Peach Bottom reactor building was considered, but none was considered for the Grand Gulf analysis. That portion of the reactor building surrounding the Grand Gulf containment is a relatively weak structure (compared with possible severe accident loadings), and it was judged to have little retention value. The decontamination factors applied in all these plants were provided by the source term expert panel and are documented in Reference E.16.

Comment: At this time, only the MELCOR code is available to the staff for source term calculation. Although it appears to be an improvement over the Source Term Code Package, it is not yet fully developed, nor is it generally available in its current form. Some method for calculating a source term will be needed by the staff and its contractors for performing or reviewing PRAs as well as other tasks (ACRS).

Response:

The MELCOR code is intended to be the staff's principal analytical model for the accident progression portions of its risk analyses. It has been used in the NUREG–1150 work (e.g., Ref. E.45) and is now being used to support other staff risk analysis work. The staff's planning for further MELCOR development, etc., is described in Reference E.40. As noted above, the staff also plans to investigate the practicality of more closely linking risk analysis calculations to codes such as MELCOR, reducing dependency on parametric models such as the XSOR codes.

E.7.2 Offsite Consequences

The review committees had a number of specific comments in the area of offsite consequence analysis. These are itemized below and staff responses provided.

Comment: The uncertainties in offsite consequences were not included in the NUREG–1150 risk uncertainty estimates (Kouts 7.2; ACRS)

Response:

As indicated in the report, it was not possible because of time constraints to include offsite consequence uncertainties in NUREG–1150. The development of needed probability distributions for parameters included in offsite consequence assessments and the incorporation of these distributions into risk uncertainty assessments is planned to be initiated in 1991.

Comment: There are also a number of uncertainties in the modeling of consequences due to decisions that would be made only during or after a severe accident. These decisions, of a sociopolitical nature, include such things as evacuation, interdiction of land and foodstuff, and the value of real property. These uncertainties have not been included in NUREG–1150, although they have been discussed elsewhere. Recent experience suggests that much lower interdiction levels than those used in NUREG–1150 are sometimes used, which would have the effect on NUREG–1150 results of increasing economic impacts and decreasing health impacts (Kouts 3.2.4, 4.12).

Response:

The staff agrees that issues such as interdiction levels actually used in the event of a reactor accident may be quite different than those used in NUREG–1150. As discussed in Chapter 2 and Appendix A, the evacuation and interdiction assumptions in NUREG–1150 were based on Environmental Protection Agency and Food and Drug Administration guidelines, respectively (Refs. E.46 and E.47). The results of sensitivity studies on these assumptions are provided in Chapters 11 and 12 of the summary report.

Comment: The MACCS code used in NUREG–1150 for offsite consequence analysis is a relatively new code, still under development. It has been neither benchmarked nor validated. Additional uncertainties are introduced by the use of such a new and relatively untested code (ACRS).

Response:

The staff agrees that the use of relatively new computer codes introduces additional uncertainty. Two efforts were undertaken as part of the NUREG–1150 project to improve the reliability of the MACCS code. These were an independent review of the chronic exposure pathway model in the code (Ref. E.48) and an independent line-by-line review of the code (Ref. E.49).

Benchmarking of the MACCS code is now under way under the auspices of an international project sponsored by the Committee on the Safety of Nuclear Installations and the Commission of the European Communities.

Comment: Important information on the offsite consequence calculations is not provided, such as the fact that inhalation doses reflect lifetime dose commitments (ANS 2.a.8.e).

Response:

In its role as a summary document, NUREG–1150 can only give a relatively brief description of the individual models used in the analysis. Detailed descriptions of the individual models are given elsewhere. For the MACCS program used to calculate offsite consequences, detailed descriptions of both the models and the computer program are given in Reference E.22. Further, the data used in the NUREG–1150 consequence calculations are described in Part 7 of Reference E.16.

E.8 Uses of NUREG–1150

The review committees had a number of specific comments in the area of the uses of NUREG–1150. These are itemized below and staff responses provided.

Comment: NUREG–1150, along with other PRAs and recent work in severe accident analysis, should be used to close out as many open issues as can reasonably be achieved and help prioritize limited research resources on the remaining safety issues. A definitive program for the use of NUREG–1150 and its supporting documents should be developed and implemented (Kouts 7.3).

The information presented in NUREG-1150 must be carefully examined in the context of the plant being studied to determine the priority ranking of safety issues, and we caution against broad generalities (ANS 6).

Use of NUREG-1150 to assist in prioritization and resolution of safety issues should be considered a priority application and a principal benefit of the substantial resources expended on this multiyear study (ANS 2.a.13.e).

Response:

As discussed in Chapter 13, the risk analyses of NUREG-1150 are intended to be used as one tool in the prioritization of research and safety issues, as well as in a number of other ways by the staff. Some applications of NUREG-1150 methods and results have already been made, such as in supporting the development of guidance for individual plant examinations (Refs. E.50 and E.51). (Chapter 13 has been updated to reflect some of the more recent uses.) As appropriately noted by the ANS comment, the plant-specific nature of the NUREG-1150 analyses should be and has been kept in mind in such applications.

Following publication of the final version of NUREG-1150, the staff intends to provide additional guidance to potential users of the report within NRC as to its strengths and weaknesses, etc.

Comment: The results of NUREG-1150 should be used only by those who have a thorough understanding of its limitations (ACRS).

Response:

The staff agrees with this comment. As noted in Section E.5.3, the staff has developed a data base and computer codes that permit the staff to modify the NUREG-1150 (and other PRA) accident frequency analyses and plans to develop similar data bases and codes for the remainder of the risk analyses. The staff intends to develop quality assurance procedures as part of this effort to minimize the potential for inappropriate calculations.

Chapter 1 has been modified to note this caution.

Comment: It is disappointing that the staff asserts that virtually no general conclusions can be drawn from a study that took almost 5 years and 17 million dollars to complete. We recommend that the Commission encourage the staff to mine more deeply the wealth of information that has been collected in the course of this study in an effort to identify generic conclusions that might be reached (ACRS).

Response:

The staff agrees that NUREG-1150 provides a substantial body of information, much of which has not yet been "mined" for use in other staff work. It is expected that this body of information will see its principal use by the staff to support the resolution of specific issues, such as study of alternative safety goals, generic issue resolution, PRA reviews, etc. The staff also intends to commit resources to the study of more general issues (e.g., the extrapolation of results for five plants to other plants).

Comment: It is recommended that the NRC issue additional guidance on the treatment of external events in the individual plant examination (IPE) process (Kouts 7.3).

Response:

Such guidance was issued in draft form (for public comment) in July 1990 (Ref. E.51).

Comment: The NUREG-1150 methodology is of special value with respect to guiding risk-reduction and risk-management actions because it makes possible a more sophisticated approach to risk management, addressing not only major contributors to risk, taken as point values, but also contributors associated with large uncertainty bands (Kouts 4.13).

Taken together with the individual plant examinations, NUREG-1150 should help guide evaluation of accident management from a risk-reduction perspective. However, such uses of NUREG-1150 would seem to be limited due to the parametric nature of the study (ANS 6).

Response:

NUREG–1150 information is being used in the development of general accident management guidance (Ref. E.52). As with the individual plant examination process, the NRC in ensuring that each licensee has developed an adequate accident management program. Such a program will be prepared by the licensee reflecting plant-specific information from a plant's individual plant examination as well as from more generic information such as NUREG–1150.

Comment: In many European countries, safety goals and objectives are related to a low risk of releases with disruptive effects on society, typically meaning releases with a potential for long-term restrictions on land usage over large areas. The summary presentations of the results in the main report do not facilitate comparisons with such alternative safety goals. An addition of such comparisons or later documentation might enhance the value of the report, especially outside the United States, since many of these may not be calculable with data in the report (Kouts 4.14).

Response:

The staff agrees that a comparison of the spectrum of national safety goals using the NUREG–1150 plant models would be of considerable interest. Such a comparison could not be accomplished in time for inclusion in NUREG–1150 but is being considered by the staff for future study.

Comment: The limited information presented in NUREG–1150 with respect to the NRC staff's proposed large-release goal would not be particularly useful in the evaluation of implementation strategies (ANS 2.a.13.d).

Response:

The staff agrees that NUREG–1150 provides very limited information on possible large-release goals and implementation strategies. The discussion provided in Chapter 13 of the report was intended as a demonstration of how NUREG–1150 risk models could be used in assessing alternative goals and applying the then-recommended definition of large release, rather than providing a definitive study of a complex technical issue. Since that time, the Commission has provided the staff with additional guidance on safety goal implementation (Ref. E.53) and possible definitions of large releases. It is expected that the NUREG–1150 models will be used by the staff as part of the further consideration of large-release definitions.

REFERENCES FOR APPENDIX E

E.1   U.S. Nuclear Regulatory Commission (USNRC), "Severe Accident Risks: An Assessment for Five U.S. Nuclear Power Plants," NUREG-1150, Second Draft for Peer Review, June 1989.

E.2   H. J. C. Kouts et al., "Special Committee Review of the Nuclear Regulatory Commission's Severe Accident Risks Report (NUREG-1150)," NUREG-1420, August 1990.

E.3   L. LeSage et al., "Report of the Special Committee on NUREG-1150, The NRC's Study of Severe Accident Risks," American Nuclear Society, June 1990.

E.4   Walston Chubb letter to Denwood F. Ross, Jr., USNRC, August 14, 1989.

E.5   Steven C. Sholly, MHB Technical Associates, letter to Denwood F. Ross, Jr., USNRC, August 7, 1989.

E.6   Roy R. Wight, State of Illinois Department of Nuclear Safety, letter to Chief, Rules and Procedures Branch, USNRC, December 15, 1989.

E.7   G. A. Hunger, Jr., Philadelphia Electric Company, letter to Chief, Rules and Procedures Branch, USNRC, January 11, 1990.

E.8   F. Coffman et al., "Human Factors Regulatory Research Program Plan," NUREG-1384, Vol. 1, October 1989.

E.9   USNRC, "Nuclear Plant Aging Research Program Plan," NUREG-1144, Revision 1, September 1987.

E.10 USNRC, "Analysis of Potential Pressurized Thermal Shock Events," *Federal Register*, Vol. 50, p. 29937, July 23, 1985.

E.11 USNRC, "Regulatory Analysis for Proposed Amendment of the PTS Rule, 10 CFR 50.61, 'Fracture Toughness Requirements for Protection Against Pressurized Thermal Shock'," cited in "Fracture Toughness Requirements For Protection Against Pressurized Thermal Shock Events," *Federal Register*, Vol. 54, p. 52946, December 26, 1989.

E.12 R. J. Breeding et al., "Evaluation of Severe Accident Risks: Surry Unit 1," Sandia National Laboratories, NUREG/CR-4551, Vol. 3, Revision 1, SAND86-1309, October 1990.

E.13 A. C. Payne, Jr., et al., "Evaluation of Severe Accident Risks: Peach Bottom Unit 2," Sandia National Laboratories, NUREG/CR-4551, Vol. 4, Revision 1, SAND86-1309, December 1990.

E.14 R. A. Chrzanowski, "March 13, 1989, letter from Cordell Reed to T. E. Murley," NRC Docket Nos. 50-295 and 50-304, August 24, 1990.

E.15 T. A. Wheeler et al., "Analysis of Core Damage Frequency from Internal Events: Expert Judgment Elicitation," Sandia National Laboratories, NUREG/CR-4550, Vol. 2, SAND86-2084, April 1989.

E.16 F. T. Harper et al., "Evaluation of Severe Accident Risks: Quantification of Major Input Parameters," Sandia National Laboratories, NUREG/CR-4551, Vol. 2, Revision 1, SAND86-1309, December 1990.

E.17 R. C. Bertucio and J. A. Julius, "Analysis of Core Damage Frequency: Surry Unit 1," Sandia National Laboratories, NUREG/CR-4550, Vol. 3, Revision 1, SAND86-2084, April 1990.

E.18 A. M. Kolaczkowski et al., "Analysis of Core Damage Frequency: Peach Bottom Unit 2," Sandia National Laboratories, NUREG/CR-4550, Vol. 4, Revision 1, SAND86-2084, August 1989.

E.19   R. C. Bertucio and S. R. Brown, "Analysis of Core Damage Frequency: Sequoyah Unit 1," Sandia National Laboratories, NUREG/CR-4550, Vol. 5, Revision 1, SAND86-2084, April 1990.

E.20   M. T. Drouin et al., "Analysis of Core Damage Frequency: Grand Gulf Unit 1," Sandia National Laboratories, NUREG/CR-4550, Vol. 6, Revision 1, SAND86-2084, September 1989.

E.21   M. B. Sattison and K. W. Hall, "Analysis of Core Damage Frequency: Zion Unit 1," Idaho National Engineering Laboratory, NUREG/CR-4550, Vol. 7, Revision 1, EGG-2554, May 1990.

E.22   D. I. Chanin, H-N Jow, J. A. Rollstin et al., "MELCOR Accident Consequence Code System (MACCS)," Sandia National Laboratories, NUREG/CR-4691, Vols. 1-3, SAND86-1562, February 1990.

E.23   USNRC, "Reactor Safety Study—An Assessment of Accident Risks in U.S. Commercial Nuclear Power Plants," WASH-1400 (NUREG-75/014), October 1975.

E.24   E. D. Gorham-Bergeron et al., "Evaluation of Severe Accident Risks: Methodology for the Accident Progression, Source Term, Consequence, Risk Integration, and Uncertainty Analyses," Sandia National Laboratories, NUREG/CR-4551, Vol. 1, Draft Revision 1, SAND86-1309, to be published.*

E.25   H. F. Martz et al., "Eliciting and Aggregating Subjective Judgments—Some Experimental Issues," *Proceedings of the 1984 Statistical Symposium on National Energy Issues* (Seattle, WA), NUREG/CP-0063, July 1985.

E.26   J. J. Gregory et al., "Evaluation of Severe Accident Risks: Sequoyah Unit 1," Sandia National Laboratories, NUREG/CR-4551, Vol. 5, Revision 1, SAND86-1309, December 1990.

E.27   T. D. Brown et al., "Evaluation of Severe Accident Risks: Grand Gulf Unit 1," Sandia National Laboratories, NUREG/CR-4551, Vol. 6, Revision 1, SAND86-1309, December 1990.

E.28   C. K. Park et al., "Evaluation of Severe Accident Risks: Zion Unit 1," Brookhaven National Laboratory, NUREG/CR-4551, Vol. 7, Draft Revision 1, BNL-NUREG-52029, to be published.*

E.29   A. D. Swain and H. E. Guttman, "Handbook of Human Reliability Analysis with Emphasis on Nuclear Power Plant Applications," Sandia National Laboratories, NUREG/CR-1278, SAND80-0200, August 1983.

E.30   E. A. Rosa et al., "Application of SLIM-MAUD: A Test of an Interactive Computer-Based Method of Organizing Expert Assessment of Human Performance and Reliability: Main Report," Brookhaven National Laboratory, NUREG/CR-4016, Vol. 1, BNL-NUREG-51828, September 1985.

E.31   D. M. Ericson, Jr., (Ed.) et al., "Analysis of Core Damage Frequency: Internal Events Methodology," Sandia National Laboratories, NUREG/CR-4550, Vol. 1, Revision 1, SAND86-2084, January 1990.

E.32   V. Ho et al., "COMPBRN III—A Computer Code for Modeling Compartment Fires," University of California at Los Angeles, UCLA-ENG-8524, November 1985.

E.33   USNRC, "Seismic Safety Research Program Plan," NUREG-1147, Revision 1, May 1987.

E.34   P. W. Baranowsky et al., "A Probabilistic Safety Analysis of DC Power Requirements for Nuclear Power Plants," NRC report NUREG-0666, April 1981.

E.35   H. D. Stewart et al., "System Analysis and Risk Assessment System (SARA), Version 4.0, Volume 1—Reference Manual," Idaho National Engineering Laboratory, NUREG/CR-5022, EGG-2522, to be published.*

E.36   K. D. Russell et al., "Integrated Reliability and Risk Analysis System (IRRAS) Version 2.0 User's Guide," Idaho National Engineering Laboratory, NUREG/CR-5111, EGG-2535, June 1990.

*Available in the NRC Public Document Room, 2120 L Street NW., Washington, DC.

E.37 J. M. Griesmeyer and L. N. Smith, "A Reference Manual for the Event Progression Analysis Code (EVNTRE)," Sandia National Laboratories, NUREG/CR–5174, SAND88–1607, September 1989.

E.38 R. L. Iman et al., "PRAMIS: Probabilistic Risk Assessment Model Integration System," Sandia National Laboratories, NUREG/CR–5262, SAND88–3093, May 1990.

E.39 USNRC, "Individual Plant Examination for Severe Accident Vulnerabilities—10 CFR § 50.54(f)," Generic Letter 88–20, November 23, 1988.

E.40 USNRC, "Revised Severe Accident Research Program Plan: FY 1990–1992," NUREG–1365, August 1989.

E.41 M. Amin et al., "An Analytical Study of Seismic Threat to Containment Integrity," Sandia National Laboratories, NUREG/CR–5098, SAND88–7018, July 1989.

E.42 P. Cybulskis, "Assessment of the XSOR Codes," Battelle Columbus Division, NUREG/CR–5346, BMI–2171, November 1989.

E.43 R. M. Summers et al., "MELCOR In–Vessel Modeling," *Proceedings of the Fifteenth Water Reactor Safety Information Meeting* (Gaithersburg, MD), NUREG/CP–0091, February 1988.

E.44 R. S. Denning et al., "Report on Radionuclide Release Calculations for Selected Severe Accident Scenarios: Supplemental Calculations," Battelle Columbus Division, NUREG/CR–4624, Vol. 6, BMI–2139, August 1990.

E.45 S. E. Dingman et al., "MELCOR Analyses for Accident Progression Issues," Sandia National Laboratories, NUREG/CR–5331, SAND89–0072, to be published.*

E.46 U. S. Environmental Protection Agency, "Manual of Protective Action Guides and Protective Actions for Nuclear Incidents," Office of Radiation Programs, Draft, 1989.

E.47 U.S. Department of Health and Human Services/Food and Drug Administration, "Accidental Radioactive Contamination of Human Food and Animal Feeds; Recommendations for State and Local Agencies," *Federal Register*, Vol. 47, No. 205, pp. 47073–47083, October 22, 1982.

E.48 U. Tveten, "Review of the Chronic Exposure Pathway Models in MACCS and Several Other Well–Known Probabilistic Risk Assessment Models," Institutt for Energiteknikk, Norway, NUREG/CR–5377, June 1990.

E.49 C. A. Dobbe et al., "Quality Assurance and Verification of the MACCS Code, Version 1.5," Idaho National Engineering Laboratory, NUREG/CR–5376, EGG–2566, February 1990.

E.50 USNRC, "Individual Plant Examination: Submittal Guidance," NUREG–1335, August 1989.

E.51 USNRC, "Procedural and Submittal Guidance for the Individual Plant Examination of External Events (IPEEE) for Severe Accident Vulnerabilities," NUREG–1407, Draft Report for Comment, July 1990.

E.52 W. J. Luckas et al., "Assessment of Candidate Accident Management Strategies," Brookhaven National Laboratory, NUREG/CR–5474, BNL–NUREG–52221, March 1990.

E.53 Samuel J. Chilk, "SECY–89–102—Implementation of the Safety Goals," Memorandum to James M. Taylor, dated June 15, 1990.

*Available in the NRC Public Document Room, 2120 L Street NW., Washington, DC.

ATTACHMENT TO

APPENDIX E

UNITED STATES
NUCLEAR REGULATORY COMMISSION
ADVISORY COMMITTEE ON REACTOR SAFEGUARDS
WASHINGTON, D. C. 20555

November 15, 1990

The Honorable Kenneth M. Carr
Chairman
U.S. Nuclear Regulatory Commission
Washington, D.C. 20555

Dear Chairman Carr:

SUBJECT: REVIEW OF NUREG-1150, "SEVERE ACCIDENT RISKS: AN
          ASSESSMENT FOR FIVE U.S. NUCLEAR POWER PLANTS"

During the 367th meeting of the Advisory Committee on Reactor
Safeguards, November 8-10, 1990, we discussed the second draft of
NUREG-1150, "Severe Accident Risks: An Assessment for Five U.S.
Nuclear Power Plants." The Committee had previously discussed this
matter with the staff and its consultants and with Dr. Herbert
Kouts, Chairman of the Special Committee to Review the Severe
Accident Risk Report. Our Subcommittees on Severe Accidents and
Probabilistic Risk Assessment discussed this report during a number
of joint meetings with members of the staff, Sandia National
Laboratories (SNL) and the American Nuclear Society (ANS) Special
Committee (Dr. Leo LeSage, Chairman). We also had the benefit of
the documents referenced.

1.   INTRODUCTION

In this report, we first offer some general comments. We then
offer recommendations concerning the publication of NUREG-1150 and
provide comments and cautions concerning interpretation or use of
some of the components of this document. And finally, we provide
more detailed comments on some key parts.

We have reviewed the reports prepared by the ANS Special Committee
and by the Special Committee to Review the Severe Accident Risk
Report appointed by the Commission and found them helpful. We have
no serious disagreements with either of these reviews, nor with
their findings.

2.   GENERAL COMMENTS

The work described in this draft of NUREG-1150 is an improvement
over that described in the first version entitled, "Reactor Risk
Reference Document." Many previously identified deficiencies in
the expert elicitation process have been corrected. The exposition
and organization of the report have been improved. The presenta-

The Honorable Kenneth M. Carr   2   November 15, 1990

tion of results is clearer. There is considerable information that was not in the original version.

The portion that deals with accident initiation and development up to the point at which core heat removal can no longer be assured is unique, compared to other contemporary PRAs, in that a method for estimating the uncertainty in the results has been developed and applied. This method and its application are significant contributions. Although the larger contributions to uncertainty in risk come from the later parts of the accident sequences, this portion is enhanced also by an extensive identification of events that can serve as accident initiators as well as an associated set of hypothesized event trees. This information should be of considerable assistance to licensees in the performance of an Individual Plant Examination (IPE). It should also be useful to plant operators and to designers.

The formulation of a more detailed representation of accident progression after severe core damage begins, and an improved description of containment performance, contribute some additional information to this important area. However, understanding of many of the physical phenomena that have an important bearing on this phase of accident progression is still very sparse, and the report may give the impression that more is known about this portion of the accident sequence than is actually the case.

The part of the sequence that begins with the release of radioactive material outside the containment is treated by a relatively new and unevaluated code system. Furthermore, there is no estimate of the uncertainties inherent in the calculations that describe this part of the sequence. Those who use the quantitative values of reported risk must recognize that these uncertainties are not accounted for in the calculated results.

3.   RECOMMENDATIONS

We recommend that the current version of NUREG-1150, with the corrections suggested by several of those who have already reviewed it in detail, be published. However, its results should be used only by those who have a thorough understanding of its limitations. Some of these limitations are discussed in subsequent sections of our report.

Since the supporting documents upon which NUREG-1150 depends could be helpful to those who perform an IPE, we recommend that these also be published as soon as feasible.

Both the Commission and the ACRS have raised questions about generic conclusions that might result from a careful examination of the results of this study. It is disappointing that the staff asserts that virtually no general conclusions can be drawn from a

The Honorable Kenneth M. Carr   3   November 15, 1990

study that took almost five years and seventeen million dollars to complete. We recommend that the Commission encourage the staff to mine more deeply the wealth of information that has been collected in the course of this study in an effort to identify generic conclusions that might be reached (see Section 5.5 of this letter).

4.   COMMENTS AND CAUTIONS CONCERNING USES OF THE MATERIAL IN NUREG-1150

We discuss below certain areas in which the methods or results should be used with caution.

4.1   Differences Among Levels of the PRA

The phenomena which contribute to sequence progression in Level 1 are generally well understood. Power plant or other related experience with system and component performance has provided sufficient data to permit predictions of sequence progression with considerably greater confidence than for those parts of the sequence described in Levels 2 and 3. NUREG-1150 is unique in the amount of effort that went into estimating uncertainties in the calculated Level 1 results. It is our view that the results of Level 1 can be used with more confidence than those of Levels 2 and 3. However, as other reviewers have reported, there are recognized deficiencies in the state-of-the-art treatments of human performance; and this report is not free of those deficiencies. In addition, some possibly important initiators, e.g., those at low power operation or at shutdown, and sequences initiated by fire, are either treated superficially or are neglected altogether.

The Level 2 analyses in NUREG-1150 include more detailed containment event trees than those found in any previous PRA. However, we have some concern that the amount of detail may lead to a conclusion that much more is known about the phenomena in this area than is actually the case.

Since there is a dearth of information concerning many of the phenomena that determine severe accident progression, expert elicitation was used most extensively in the Level 2 portion of the PRAs. There is general agreement that the techniques used for eliciting expert opinion in preparation of the second draft were significantly better than those used for the first draft. However, with insufficient information there can be no experts. Thus, use of the term "expert opinion" in a description of some of the Level 2 work may be misleading. (Further comments about the expert elicitation process are given in Section 5.3). We applaud efforts to improve on the Level 2 treatment of previous PRAs. We nevertheless believe that the results from Level 2 presented in this latest draft must be regarded as having major uncertainties in both calculated mean values and in estimated uncertainties.

The Honorable Kenneth M. Carr   4   November 15, 1990

The MELCOR Accident Consequence Code System (MACCS) was used for the consequence calculations of Level 3. Use of MACCS is a departure from many existing PRAs that use the Calculation of Reactor Accident Consequences (CRAC) series of codes. MACCS is a relatively new code, still under development. It has been neither benchmarked nor validated. Thus, in addition to the uncertainties inherent in the physical phenomena that enter into consequence modeling, additional uncertainties are introduced by the use of a new and relatively untested code.

No effort was made to estimate the uncertainties in the Level 3 calculations. Thus, the estimates of uncertainties in risk that are given in the report are only those arising from the uncertainties calculated for Levels 1 and 2. It is our judgment that the uncertainties in modeling the consequences of a release can be at least as large as those estimated for Level 2. For example, the health effects, especially for low dose exposures, are subject to large uncertainty, and the exposures themselves depend on actions (e.g., evacuation, sheltering, interdiction of land and crops) for which the uncertainty in prediction is largely unknown.

4.2 Assumptions Made in Screening

Users of the report should be aware of the assumptions made in the screening process for low-probability, high-consequence events. For example, the analysts assumed that the probability of total loss of DC power was less than 1×10^{-7} per year and thus could be neglected. The same assumption was made for loss of all service water. Thus, those who use the results in IPE work should recognize that these assumptions may not be valid for all operating plants.

4.3 Credit for Decay Heat Removal by Feed and Bleed

The success of the feed and bleed operation is highly dependent on human performance. Everyone seems to agree that there are large uncertainties in its treatment in this report. In addition, it is likely that the performance of valves, which must function if this maneuver is to be successful, are not well represented by the data for valve performance used in the calculations.

4.4 Performance of Motor-Operated Valves

There is now a significant body of evidence which indicates that the failure probability used to describe the operation of certain key motor-operated valves is too low. This may have an important bearing on the outcome of several accident sequences described in the report.

The Honorable Kenneth M. Carr   5   November 15, 1990

4.5 Contribution of Pump-Seal Failure to the Risk of Small Break LOCAs

We believe that more recent information and some new seal designs developed since the study was made would lead to a prediction of risk less than that reported.

4.6 Containment Performance

The lack of information about many of the physical phenomena that determine the performance of a containment system in a severe accident situation is such that only educated guesses can be made for some sequences that might make significant contributions to risk. Although the large number of event trees developed in the containment analyses is indicative of what was hypothesized by the analysts, the amount and quality of information concerning a number of key phenomena that determine behavior at branch points are low. The difficulty of arriving at a result with significant confidence is illustrated by two examples. In the analysis of the performance of the Mark I containment used in early BWRs, the experts in the original study predicted a large conditional probability of early failure. In the second study a different group of experts produced a bimodal distribution because part of the panel concluded that the probability of early failure was high, and part considered it low. A second example is the calculation of risk produced by postulated direct containment heating (DCH). In the first study, the calculated risk due to DCH for PWRs with large dry containments was a major contributor to the total risk. In the second version, its contribution was significantly less. In neither case had there been a major change in the information about relevant physical phenomena available at the time of the first study. Further, we find no consideration of the impact of ex-vessel steam explosions on early containment failure. There is little unambiguous guidance here for a licensee performing an IPE.

5. AREAS FOR SPECIAL COMMENT

In this section, we provide more detailed comments on some areas that appear to us to deserve special attention.

5.1 Fire Risk

The fire contribution to core-damage probability was estimated for two plants using insights gained during previous fire PRAs and studies, the latest methods and data bases developed under NRC sponsorship, and the benefits of extensive plant walkdowns. The methods and data used were probably the best available at the time the reported work was performed. Nevertheless we conclude, on the basis of later information, that the results should be viewed as being incomplete. The models used were not able to take full account of several issues identified by SNL in a scoping study of

The Honorable Kenneth M. Carr   6   November 15, 1990

fire risks that was completed more recently. These are issues that have not been adequately considered in past fire risk studies and may increase the risk. Of particular concern are seismic-fire interactions, adequacy of fire barriers, equipment survival in the environment generated by the fire, and control systems interactions. The PRA for the LaSalle nuclear plant, which is nearing completion, may provide insights concerning the risk importance of these issues.

5.2 Seismic Risk

The seismic PRAs for the Surry and Peach Bottom nuclear plants were performed using two quite different representations of the seismic hazards. The results however, at least for sequences leading to core damage, were similar in terms of which accident initiators and sequences were important. This tends to support the acceptability of using the seismic margin approach rather than a PRA in the search for plant-specific seismic vulnerabilities in the IPE-External Events (IPEEE) program. However, the success of either approach in finding vulnerabilities depends strongly on walkdowns to identify those systems and components to be evaluated. Knowledge of what to look for is derived chiefly from PRAs done on other plants, and these have tended to focus primarily on core damage rather than releases of radioactive material to the environment. Although containments are usually quite rugged seismically, this is not necessarily true for containment cooling systems, containment isolation systems, etc.

Although the two seismic PRAs in NUREG-1150 have been carried through Level 3, these results have not been reported. We believe that these results might provide valuable insights about seismic vulnerabilities of containment systems.

5.3 The Expert Elicitation Process

There is general agreement that the use of expert elicitation in the preparation of the results in this draft of the report is improved compared to that used for the first version. However, we have reservations about some parts of the application of the process. For example, during our discussions of the choice of the participating experts we got the impression that an effort was made to choose participants in such a way that a wide spectrum of viewpoints would be represented. This was defended as proper, based on the assumption that unless this wide spectrum of opinion was represented, the uncertainty in expert opinion would not be appropriately accounted for. We found this argument unconvincing, and would have preferred to see individuals chosen primarily on the basis of their knowledge and understanding of the phenomena being considered. Furthermore, we were told that the budget for the study provided only enough funding to support the participation of about 20 percent of the experts who served on the panels. The

The Honorable Kenneth M. Carr   7   November 15, 1990

remainder were drawn from the NRC staff or from organizations with contractual relationships to the NRC. This biased the selection toward people whose organizations depend upon the NRC for support. We also observe that the membership of the panels seems to have been dominated by analysts in contrast to those who have done significant research on phenomena of importance to the accident sequences being described.

5.4 Source Term Description

The staff, or at least that part of it closely associated with this study, has discarded for future use the Source Term Code Package (STCP) that was one of the resources used by the expert panels in the preparation of NUREG-1150. The expert elicitation method is too resource intensive to be used generally. At this time, only the MELCOR code is available to the staff for source term calculation. Although it appears to be an improvement over the STCP, it is not yet fully developed, nor is it generally available in its current form. Some method for calculating a source term will be needed by the staff and its contractors for performing or reviewing PRAs, as well as for other tasks, such as a revision of the siting rule.

5.5 Lack of General Conclusions

We have asked the staff whether the results reported in NUREG-1150 shed any light on the risk expected due to operation of the population of plants now licensed. With few exceptions, it is the staff's view that one can tell little or nothing about the expected risk of plants not studied from the results of the study of these five plants in NUREG-1150. In spite of these statements, however, those who prepared the report propose that applications will include evaluation and resolution of generic issues and prioritization of future research and prioritization of inspection activities. If, as we were told, the results from the analyses of these plants have little or no generic significance, application of these results must be made with considerable caution.

We believe that the large amount of information collected as input to the calculations made during this study, and the results of the large number of analyses undertaken, must surely permit some more general conclusions to be drawn than we find in this report. For example, the risk calculated for each of the five plants analyzed (although calculated only for internal initiators) falls within the Quantitative Health Objectives (QHOs) set forth in the Safety Goal Policy Statement. Each was designed and constructed and, is operating within the rules and regulations promulgated by the Commission. There must be some significance in the fact that plants supplied by a number of different vendors, constructed at different locations, under supervision of different organizations, over a period of more than a decade, with rather different balance

Appendix E

The Honorable Kenneth M. Carr   8   November 15, 1990

of plant configurations, and different containments, nevertheless fall within the QHOs. Is application of the NRC's regulations achieving the objectives of the NRC Safety Goal Policy?

Another area of interest is the risk reduction achieved by some recently promulgated rules. The report indicates that station blackout is a significant risk contributor for three of the plants studied. Answers to questions we asked during our meetings with the staff indicated that some of the plants analyzed had implemented most of the requirements of the Station Blackout Rule, while others had only just begun the process. Could one draw any conclusions from the plants studied as to the risk reduction to be expected from implementation of the Station Blackout Rule? Or could one estimate the risk reduction for some "average" plant? This would be interesting, since in the typical cost benefit analysis associated with backfit it is assumed that some such conclusion can be drawn about plants generally. It would be useful to see what an examination of these five plants would indicate.

The five nuclear power plants chosen for the study were selected partly on the basis of the different types of containment represented. We find little or no discussion of relative containment performance or identification of containment designs that might be expected to have superior mitigation capabilities. For example, in light of the containment being proposed for the Advanced Boiling Water Reactor (ABWR), it would be helpful to have any information or conclusions that were developed during the course of the study as to relative efficacy of the containment being proposed for that design as compared to the Mark I or the Mark III containments. Or, for large dry containments, does the subatmospheric operation of the Surry system provide a substantial decrease in risk (because, for example, of its continuous indication of leak tightness) as compared to a large dry containment operated at atmospheric pressure?

Although it may not be feasible to make major changes in containments of reactors now in operation, it is possible to choose containments with superior mitigation characteristics for nuclear plants not yet constructed. It might even be feasible, as a result of the study, to recommend a containment design that combines the best features of several of the existing systems. If in the course of this study information has been developed that could be used to reduce the conditional failure probability of containment, given severe core damage, the risk uncertainty in new designs might be

NUREG-1150   EA-8

The Honorable Kenneth M. Carr   9   November 15, 1990

reduced without requiring any additional studies of core damage progression.

Sincerely,

Carlyle Michelson
Chairman

References:

1.   U.S. Nuclear Regulatory Commission, NUREG-1150, "Severe Accident Risks: An Assessment for Five U.S. Nuclear Power Plants," Volumes 1 and 2 (Second Draft for Peer Review), dated June 1989.

2.   American Nuclear Society, "Report of the Special Committee on NUREG-1150, The NRC's Study of Severe Accident Risks," L. LeSage (Chairman), dated August 1990.

3.   U.S. Nuclear Regulatory Commission, NUREG-1420, "Special Committee Review of the Nuclear Regulatory Commission's Severe Accident Risks Report (NUREG-1150)," H. Kouts (Chairman), dated August 1990.

4.   U.S. Nuclear Regulatory Commission, NUREG-1150, "Reactor Risk Reference Document," Volumes 1, 2, and 3, Draft issued for comment, dated February 1987.

NRC FORM 335 (2–89) NRCM 1102, 3201, 3202	U.S. NUCLEAR REGULATORY COMMISSION **BIBLIOGRAPHIC DATA SHEET** (See instructions on the reverse)	1. REPORT NUMBER (Assigned by NRC, Add Vol., Supp., Rev., and Addendum Num- bers, if any.) NUREG–1150 Vol. 3

2. TITLE AND SUBTITLE

Severe Accident Risks: An Assessment for Five U.S. Nuclear Power Plants

Appendices D and E
Final Report

3. DATE REPORT PUBLISHED

MONTH	YEAR
January	1991

4. FIN OR GRANT NUMBER

5. AUTHOR(S)

6. TYPE OF REPORT

Final Technical

7. PERIOD COVERED (Inclusive Dates)

8. PERFORMING ORGANIZATION – NAME AND ADDRESS (If NRC, provide Division, Office or Region, U.S. Nuclear Regulatory Commission, and mailing address; if contractor, provide name and mailing address.)

Division of Systems Research
Office of Nuclear Regulatory Research
U.S. Nuclear Regulatory Commission
Washington, DC 20555

9. SPONSORING ORGANIZATION – NAME AND ADDRESS (If NRC, type "Same as above"; if contractor, provide NRC Division, Office or Region, U.S. Nuclear Regulatory Commission, and mailing address.)

Same as 8. above.

10. SUPPLEMENTARY NOTES

11. ABSTRACT (200 words or less)

This report summarizes an assessment of the risks from severe accidents in five commercial nuclear power plants in the United States. These risks are measured in a number of ways, including: the estimated frequencies of core damage accidents from internally initiated accidents, and externally initiated accidents for two of the plants; the performance of containment structures under severe accident loadings; the potential magnitude of radionuclide releases and offsite consequences of such accidents; and the overall risk (the product of accident frequencies and consequences). Supporting this summary report are a large number of reports written under contract to NRC which provide the detailed discussion of the methods used and results obtained in these risk studies.

Volume 3 of this report contains two appendices. Appendix D summarizes comments received and staff responses on the first (February 1987) draft of NUREG–1150. Appendix E provides a similar summary of comments and responses, but for the second (June 1989) version of the report.

12. KEY WORDS/DESCRIPTORS (List words or phrases that will assist researchers in locating the report.)

severe accidents
risk analysis
probabilistic risk analysis

13. AVAILABILITY STATEMENT

Unlimited

14. SECURITY CLASSIFICATION

(This Page)

Unclassified

(This Report)

Unclassified

15. NUMBER OF PAGES

16. PRICE

NRC FORM 335 (2–89)

www.ingramcontent.com/pod-product-compliance
Lightning Source LLC
Chambersburg PA
CBHW080317290526
45790CB00005B/2073